Direct Hits Core Vocabulary of the SAT: Volume 1

By Larry Krieger

Edited by Ted Griffith

This copy belongs to:

AVN

For more information, contact us at:

Direct Hits Publishing
2639 Arden Rd., Atlanta GA 30327
Info@DirectHitsEducation.com

Visit our website at:
www.DirectHitsEducation.com

First Edition: August 2008

ISBN 10:   0-981-81840-4

ISBN 13:   978-0-9818184-0-5

Library of Congress Control Number: 2008932920

Edited by Ted Griffith

Cover Design by Carlo da Silva

Interior Design by Katherine Goodman

Acknowledgements

This book would not have been possible without the help of great students, dedicated friends and a tireless Product Manager. I would like to thank the following students for their valuable suggestions: Jacob Byrne, Jill Reid, Lindsey Brenner, Misha Milijanic, and Britney Frankel. Special thanks to Lauren Treene, Evan Hewel, Holland McTyeire and Alex Washington for their ability to help me connect vivid movie scenes with difficult SAT words.

I would also like to thank Jane Armstrong for her unfailing enthusiasm and Jan Altman for her original research. Extra special thanks to Claire Griffith for her encouragement and creative ideas and to Luther Griffith for his keen insights and impeccable judgment.

This book would not have been possible without a dedicated Product Manager. Ted Griffith has been everything an author could ask for - resourceful, innovative and meticulous.

And finally, I am deeply grateful for the "close reads," patience and love of my wife, Susan.

Table of Contents

Introduction

Have you ever visited a country where the people spoke a language you didn't understand? If you have had this experience, you may have vivid memories of misreading signs, ordering wrong foods, and feeling frustrated by not understanding what is going on around you.

Many students complain that taking the PSAT and the SAT is like trying to understand a foreign language. The critical reading and sentence completion questions do contain a number of difficult words. For example, recent SATs included many challenging words such as acquiesce.

Although these words may seem obscure, they are actually everyday words that appear in newspapers, books, and even movies. For example, in "Pirates of the Caribbean: The Curse of the Black Pearl," Elizabeth Swann and Captain Barbossa conduct negotiations that include the word acquiesce. Although he claims to be a "humble pirate," Captain Barbossa does understand what the "long word" acquiesce means. He firmly rejects Swann's demands saying, "I'm disinclined to acquiesce to your request. Means no!"

Why is having a rich vocabulary that includes words such as acquiesce important? Words are among our most valuable tools for learning and communicating. As your vocabulary increases, you will become more articulate. As an articulate person, you will be able to speak more eloquently and write more convincingly.

Introduction

Researchers have shown that a superior vocabulary is strongly associated with success in school, business, the professions and standardized tests such as the PSAT and SAT.

Learning new words doesn't have to be a grim chore. I believe that augmenting your vocabulary can be fun. I've selected 365 challenging words – one for each day of the year – that have appeared on recent SATs. The first 190 are in this volume and the second 175 words are in Volume 2. Each word is illustrated with vivid examples taken from popular movies, TV shows, and famous historic events. This mix of pop culture and history is based upon the old childhood rhyme that, "what's learned with pleasure is learned full measure."

I hope you enjoy learning the vocabulary words in Volume I. I also want you to test your ability to use these words. Each SAT includes 19 sentence completion questions worth 35 percent of your Critical Reading score. You'll find a set of 10 sentence completion questions at the end of each chapter. They will give you an opportunity to test your vocabulary on SAT questions. Answers and a detailed explanation of each question follow each set of questions.

So what are you waiting for? Turn to the first two pages. You'll find Emperor Commodus ("Gladiator"), Vernon Dursley (*Harry Potter and the Sorcerer's Stone*) and Winston Churchill all waiting and eager to help you augment your vocabulary!

About Larry Krieger

Larry Krieger is one of the foremost SAT experts in the country. His renowned teaching methods and SAT prep courses are praised for both their inventive, engaging approaches and their results. Students under Krieger's guidance improve their SAT scores by an average of 200 points.

Formerly a social studies supervisor and AP Art History teacher at New Jersey's SAT powerhouse Montgomery Township High School near Princeton, Krieger led the school to a Number 1 ranking in the state and nation for a comprehensive public high school. In 2004, Montgomery students achieved a record national average score of 629 on the Critical Reading section of the SAT.

Beginning in 2005, the College Board recognized Krieger's AP Art History course as the "strongest in the world" for three straight years. With an open enrollment, 60% of the senior class took the course and 100% made grades of 3 or higher, including some special education students.

Krieger is the co-author of several US History, World History and AP Art History texts used throughout the country. He earned a BA in History and an MAT from University of North Carolina at Chapel Hill, and has an MA in Sociology from Wake Forest.

Though Krieger admits to being completely unprepared for his first SAT in high school, he regularly takes the SAT to keep up with changes on the new test.

Chapter 1

CORE VOCABULARY I: 1–50

The English language contains just over one million words – the most of any language in human history. If each of these words had an equal chance of being used on the SAT, studying for the test would be a truly impossible task.

Fortunately, the pool of words used by Educational Testing Service (ETS) test writers is actually relatively small. Many key words are repeatedly tested. This is particularly true of Level 3 and 4 words that over half of the test-takers (students like you!) do not know. These words are crucial to achieving a high Critical Reading score.

These crucial mid-level words form the core vocabulary you need to know to score well on the Critical Reading portion of the SAT. Based upon a careful analysis of recent tests, we have identified 100 Core Vocabulary Words. The first 50 of these words are in Chapter 1 and the second 50 are in Chapter 2. The division is arbitrary. Each word is a high frequency word that you absolutely, positively must know.

CORE VOCABULARY I: 1–50

1. AMBIVALENT:
Contradictory, having mixed feelings

In the movie "Gladiator," Emperor Commodus is AMBIVALENT about giving the order to kill Maximus at the Coliseum. He wants to eliminate a hated rival. At the same time, he also wants to please the pro-Maximus crowd that is cheering for their triumphant gladiator.

In the movie "The Notebook," Allie has to choose between Noah and Lon. She is emotionally torn by her AMBIVALENT feelings as she tells Noah, "There is no easy way, no matter what I do, somebody gets hurt." She later reiterates her AMBIVALENT feelings when she tells Lon, "When I'm with Noah I feel like one person and when I'm with you I feel like someone totally different."

2. ANOMALY:
Deviation from the norm, something that is ATYPICAL

In the Harry Potter series, Vernon Dursley prides himself on being "perfectly normal, thank you very much." An ANOMALY is the last thing Dursley wants in his life. In the opening chapter of *Harry Potter and the Sorcerer's Stone*, however, Dursley notices several strange ANOMALIES or what he calls "funny stuff." For example, he spots a cat that appears to be reading a map. He also notices a number of odd people who are dressed in colorful robes. And that is not all: flocks of owls can be seen flying during the daytime.

3. SARCASTIC and SARDONIC:
Mocking, derisive comments that taunt and sting

Winston Churchill was famous for his SARCASTIC and SARDONIC comments. Here are two well-known examples:

Bessie Braddock:	Sir, you are a drunk.
Churchill:	Madame, you are ugly. In the morning I shall be sober, and you will still be ugly.
Nancy Astor:	Sir, if you were my husband I would give you poison.
Churchill:	If I were your husband I would take it.

4. DEARTH and PAUCITY:
A scarcity or shortage of something

In her book *Silent Spring* (1962), Rachael Carson warned that the indiscriminate use of synthetic pesticides such as DDT was a threat to wildlife and especially birds. Carson's GRAPHIC (very vivid) description of the growing DEARTH of robins and PAUCITY of other songbirds sparked a public outcry that led to the banning of most uses of DDT.

5. PRATTLE:
To speak in a foolish manner, to babble incessantly

In the movie "Office Space," Milton continuously PRATTLES to himself about how he is abused by management and how his co-workers repeatedly borrow his stapler. Here is an example of Milton PRATTLING on and on:

> *"I don't care if they lay me off either, because I told, I told Bill that if they move my desk one more time, then, then, I'm, I'm quitting, I'm going to quit. And, I told Don too, because they've moved my desk four times already this year, and I used to be over by the window, and I could see the squirrels, and they were married, but then, they switched from the Swingline to the Boston stapler, but I kept my Swingline stapler because it didn't bind up as much, and I kept the staplers for the Swingline stapler and it's not okay, because if they take my stapler then I'll set the building on fire ..."*

6.   WRY:

Dry, humorous with a clever twist and a touch of irony

Seth Cohen ("The O.C.") and Chandler ("Friends") are both known for their WRY sense of humor. Here are two examples:

Seth:	What happens in Mexico, stays in Mexico.
Ryan:	What happens in Mexico?
Seth:	I don't know, because it stays there. That's why we have to go!
Ross:	I'm going on a trip to China!
Joey:	Wow, you'll get to eat lots of Chinese food.
Chandler:	Or as they call it – food.

7. **UNCONVENTIONAL and UNORTHODOX:**
Not ordinary or typical; characterized by avoiding customary conventions and behaviors

In "High School Musical," Zeke, Martha and the Skaterdude all have UNCONVENTIONAL passions. Zeke is a basketball star who loves to bake. Martha is a brainiac who loves hip hop. And the Skaterdude is a slacker who loves to play the cello. Needless to say, their friends are initially aghast and express their disapproval of this unusual and UNCONVENTIONAL behavior in this rousing chorus:

> *No, no, no, noooooooooooo*
> *No, no, no*
> *Stick to the stuff you know*
> *If you wanna be cool*
> *Follow one simple rule*
> *Don't mess with the status quo!*

8. **PAINSTAKING and METICULOUS:**
Extremely careful; very exacting

Michelangelo's Pieta is recognized as one of the world's greatest artistic masterpieces. In 1972 a mentally disturbed man named Laszio Toth walked into Saint Peter's Cathedral and attacked the Pieta with a hammer. Experts METICULOUSLY gathered each broken fragment and PAINSTAKINGLY restored the work. Today, the Pieta is protected by a bullet-proof acrylic glass panel.

9. AUDACIOUS:
Fearlessly, often recklessly daring; very bold

What do Ben Campbell ("21") and Tony Stark ("Iron Man") have in common? Both conceive and execute AUDACIOUS plans. Ben is a math whiz who joins a secret team of equally brilliant math students who AUDACIOUSLY plan to use card counting and an intricate system of hand signals to win a fortune from Las Vegas casinos. Tony is a wealthy industrialist and master engineer who is captured by Afghan terrorists and ordered to build a deadly missile. Instead, he AUDACIOUSLY builds an impregnable iron suit that is equipped with advanced weapons. Tony's AUDAC-IOUS plan works and he successfully overpowers his captors and escapes.

10. INDIFFERENT and APATHETIC:
Marked by a lack of interest or concern

In the movie "Ferris Bueller's Day Off," the economics teacher Ben Stein explains that "in the Republican-controlled House of Representatives, in an effort to ALLEVIATE (Word 31) the effects of the ... Anyone? Anyone?" But his students are INDIFFERENT and ignore his question. Stein continues asking questions but his efforts are FUTILE (Word 46). Some students are so APATHETIC that they fall asleep.

11. DIFFIDENT:
Lacking self-confidence; self-effacing; NOT assertive

What do Sarah ("Save the Last Dance"), Peter Parker ("Spider-Man") and Milton ("Office Space") have in common? All three were originally very DIFFIDENT. However, all three were able to overcome their DIFFIDENCE. Sarah became a great dancer, Peter Parker became Spider-Man and Milton became a wealthy man after burning down Initech and finding checks worth over $300,000.

12.   PRAGMATIC:
Practical; sensible; NOT idealistic or romantic

Do you believe in love at first sight? A romantic or IDEALISTIC person probably would believe in true love and love's first kiss. In contrast, a PRAGMATIC person would want to test his or her feelings by dating and even living together.

In the movie "Enchanted," Giselle is rescued by Robert Philip. Unlike the romantic Giselle, Robert is a PRAGMATIC divorce lawyer who does not believe in love at first sight. Ever the PRAGMATIST, Robert has been dating his girlfriend for five years.

13.   EVOCATION:
An imaginative re-creation

What do the treasures of Pharaoh Tutankhamen, Jamie Foxx's portrayal of Ray Charles in the movie "Ray" and the movie "Titanic" all have in common? They are all powerful EVOCATIONS. The treasures of Pharaoh Tutankhamen are EVOCATIONS of the power and splendor of Ancient Egypt. Jamie Foxx's portrayal of Ray Charles is a vivid EVOCATION of the life and times of the legendary blues singer. And the movie "Titanic" is a remarkable EVOCATION of what it was like to be a passenger on the great but doomed ship.

14. **PRESUMPTUOUS:**
    Overbearing; impertinently bold; character-ized by brashly overstepping ones place

In the movie "300," Queen Gorgo boldly told the Persian envoy, "Do not be coy or stupid, Persian. You can afford neither in Sparta." Queen Gorgo's willing-ness to speak out astonished the Persian envoy. Shocked by the Spartan Queen's PRESUMPTUOUS statement, the envoy questioned, "What makes this woman think she can speak among men?"

15. **RECALCITRANT:**
    Marked by stubborn resistance to and defiance of authority or guidance; obstinate; OBDURATE

What do Hester Prynne (*The Scarlet Letter*) and the singer Amy Winehouse have in common? Both are RECALCITRANT. In *The Scarlet Letter*, the Reverend Wilson demanded that Hester reveal the name of the father of her child. But Hester was RECALCITRANT. Despite "the heavy weight of a thousand eyes, all fastened upon her," Hester stubbornly refused to name the father defiantly declaring, "Never...I will not speak!" In her song "Rehab," Amy Winehouse is also defiantly RECALCITRANT. Her friends and family all beg her to go to rehab, but Amy is OBDURATE and defiantly declares, "No, no, no."

16. BOON:
A timely benefit; blessing

BANE:
A source of harm and ruin

Fifty Cent was shot 9 times and lived! Was the shooting a BANE or a BOON for his career? At first it was a BANE because the pain was excruciating, and Fiddy had to spend weeks in a hospital recuperating. But the shooting turned out to be a BOON for his career because it gave Fiddy "street cred" and lots of publicity.

17. CLANDESTINE and SURREPTITIOUS:
Secret; covert; not open; NOT ABOVEBOARD

What do the Men in Black ("Men In Black"), Dumbledore's Army (*Harry Potter and the Order of the Phoenix*) and Sector Seven ("Transformers") all have in common? They are all CLANDESTINE groups that conduct SURREPTITIOUS activities. The Men in Black SURREPTITIOUSLY regulate alien life forms on Earth. Dumbledore's Army teaches Hogwart's students how to defend themselves against the Dark Arts. And Sector Seven guards the mysterious All Spark and keeps the body of Megatron permanently frozen.

18. AFFABLE, AMIABLE, GENIAL, GREGARIOUS:
All mean agreeable; marked by a pleasing personality; warm and friendly

What do talk show host Jay Leno ("The Tonight Show"), NBA superstar LeBron James and fairy tale princess Giselle ("Enchanted") have in common? All three are known for their AFFABLE personalities. Jay Leno's GENIAL personality puts his guests at ease, thus creating a warm and friendly atmosphere. LeBron James' GREGARIOUS personality has made him a fan favorite both on and off the court. And in the movie "Enchanted," the AMIABLE Giselle exudes a natural goodness and pleasing personality that charms normally ill-tempered New Yorkers and even captivates the PRAGMATIC (Word 12) Robert Philip.

19. CONFOUNDED:
Puzzled; confused; bewildered; very
PERPLEXED

The movie "Cloverfield" opens with a group of friends enjoying "the best night ever" at a surprise party in Manhattan. But their party is suddenly interrupted when the building shakes, the lights flicker and thunderous explosions roar in the distance. They race to the roof and are stunned to see buildings exploding and, most incredibly of all, the head of the Statue of Liberty crashing on the street below. Like everyone else, the group is frightened and CONFOUNDED. What is happening? Who or what is attacking the city? What should they do? What can they do?

20. PRODIGIOUS:
Huge; massive; enormous

What do the waves at Mavericks, California and the blue whale have in common? Both are PRODIGIOUS. Following a winter storm, waves at Mavericks routinely crest at over 25 feet while the most PRODIGIOUS top out at over 50 feet. Although they are not big wave surfers, blue whales are PROD-IGIOUS. The largest animal to ever live on our planet, the blue whale can weigh as much as 200 tons and grow to 80 feet in length. The blue whale's PRODIGIOUS tongue is as large as an elephant and its PRODIGIOUS heart is the size of a car.

21. AMBIGUOUS:

Unclear; uncertain; open to more than one interpretation; not definitive

The final scene of the TV drama "The Sopranos" was deliberately AMBIGUOUS. Tony Soprano, his wife Carmela and their son AJ are eating onion rings in a local diner as the jukebox plays the Journey song, "Don't Stop Believin'." One man, possibly an assassin, has previously left the table and entered the nearby restroom. Meanwhile, Tony's daughter, Meadow, is about to enter the diner. A black screen suddenly appears abruptly ending the scene and the series. What will happen next? Will Tony greet his daughter or be shot? We don't know, because the ending is AMBIGUOUS.

22. REPROACH:

To express disapproval; scold; rebuke; CENSURE

In this classic scene from "Billy Madison," Ms. Vaughn REPROACHES Billy for making fun of a 3rd grade student who is having trouble reading:

3rd Grader:	Wa-wa-wa-once th-th-th-th-there wa-wa-wa-was a-a-a-a g-g-girl

Billy Madison:	Kid can't even read.
Ernie:	Cut it out dude, you're gonna get us in trouble.
Billy Madison:	T-T-T-Today Junior!
Billy Madison:	OW! You're tearing my ear off!
Veronica Vaughn:	Making fun of a little kid for trying to read. Are you psycho? Do you not have a soul? You keep your mouth shut for the next two weeks or I'm going to fail you. End of story.

23. NOSTALGIA:
A sentimental longing for the past

The power of NOSTALGIA can be seen in the number of bands that have reunited for reunion tours. Reunited bands include Stone Temple Pilots (split in 2003), New Kids on the Block (split in 1994) and such recently re-energized bands as the B-52s, the Black Crowes, the Police and Motley Crue. The bands and their adoring fans recapture a feeling of NOSTALGIA by singing old songs and reliving great moments from a time when they were younger.

24. CONJECTURE:
An inference based upon guesswork; a SUPPOSITION

What do paleontologist Dr. Ross Geller ("Friends") and celebrity columnist Perez Hilton have in common? Both routinely make CONJECTURES. Lacking hard evidence, Ross must make CON-

JECTURES about how dinosaurs communicated with each other. Similarly, Perez Hilton often must make SUPPOSITIONS about who Britney Spears is dating, which star is expecting a child, which celebrity couple is getting married and who has adopted another child.

25. OBSOLETE:
No longer in use; outmoded in design or style

What do the typewriter, mimeograph machine and walkman all have in common? Although once UBIQUITOUS (Word 48) in offices and homes across America, all three machines are now OBSOLETE. The computer's word processing capabilities have replaced the typewriter, the high-speed photocopier has replaced the mimeograph machine and the iPod has replaced the walkman.

26. AUSPICIOUS:
Very favorable

How long would you wait to marry your true love? The Mogul princes of India were required to wait until the emperor's astrologers felt that all of the planetary signs were AUSPICIOUS. For example, they required Crown Prince Shah Jahan and Mumtaz Mahal to postpone their wedding date for five years. During that time, the lovers were not allowed to see one another. The long-awaited wedding finally took place when all of the astrological signs were AUSPICIOUS. The signs must have indeed been AUSPICIOUS because the royal couple enjoyed 19 years of marital joy and happiness.

27. MOROSE:

Very depressed, DESPONDENT (Word 175), mournful

During their 19 years together, Mumtaz Mahal gave Emperor Shah Jahan fourteen children. When she suddenly died during childbirth, Shah Jahan was grief-stricken. The now MOROSE emperor canceled all appointments and refused to eat or drink for eight days. One historian recorded that when Mumtaz Mahal died, the emperor "was in danger to die himself." When he finally recovered, Shah Jahan built the Taj Mahal as a mausoleum for his beloved wife.

28. IMPASSE:

A deadlock; stalemate; failure to reach an agreement

The Constitutional Convention was almost totally de-railed by an IMPASSE between the large states and the small states. Led by Virginia, the large states demanded that representation in both houses of Congress should be based on population. The small states, led by New Jersey, countered with a plan calling for equal representation in a unicameral Congress. As tempers rose, the IMPASSE appeared to be INSURMOUNTABLE (Word 185). However, the delegates successfully broke the IMPASSE by agreeing to a Great Compromise that created a bi-cameral, or two-house, Congress with equal representation in the Senate and representation based upon population in the House.

29. ANACHRONISM:

The false assignment of an event, person, scene or language to a time when the event, person, scene, or word did not exist

Northern Renaissance artists often included ANACHRONISMS in their paintings. For example, "Last Supper" by the 15th Century artist Dirk Bouts shows Christ and his disciples eating in a royal palace in what is today Belgium. While the ANACHRONISM in Bouts' painting is deliberate, the ANACHRONISMS in modern movies are unplanned blunders. For example, in the Civil War movie "Glory," a digital watch is clearly visible on the wrist of a boy waving goodbye to the black soldiers of the 54th Massachusetts Regiment. And in the movie "Gladiator," you can see a gas cylinder in the back of one of the overturned "Roman" chariots!

30. BELIE:

To give a false impression; to contradict

In the movie "Ten Things I Hate About You," Kat composed a poem expressing her feelings about Patrick. As she began reading the poem to her literature class, her rhymes reflected her anger:

> *I hate the way you talk to me,*
> *And the way you cut your hair.*
> *I hate the way you drive my car.*
> *I hate it when you stare.*
> *I hate your big dumb combat boots,*
> *And the way you read my mind.*
> *I hate you so much it makes me sick;*
> *It even makes me rhyme.*

But then Kat's eyes filled with tears as she read the following lines from her poem:

> *I hate it when you're not around,*
> *And the fact that you didn't call.*
> *But mostly I hate the way I don't hate you.*
> *Not even close, not even a little bit,*
> *Not even at all.*

Kat's poem BELIED her true feelings about Patrick. Although she said she hated him, Kat actually really liked Patrick.

31. MITIGATE, MOLLIFY, ASSUAGE, ALLEVIATE:
All mean to relieve; lessen; to ease

Did you know that almost half of all Americans take at least one prescription pill every day? Americans use pills to MITIGATE the symptoms of everything from migraine headaches to acid indigestion.

Stephen Douglas believed that the doctrine of popular sovereignty would MOLLIFY, or lessen popular passions about, the extension of slavery into the territories. But Douglas badly misjudged the public mood in the North. Instead of MOLLIFYING the public, popular sovereignty inflamed passions and helped propel the nation toward the Civil War.

32. COVET:
To strongly desire; to crave

What do Lord Voldemort (*Harry Potter and the Deathly Hallows*), The Wicked Witch of the West ("Wizard of Oz") and Megatron ("Transformers") all have in common? All three are villains who COVET something they can't have but desperately want. Lord Voldemort COVETS the Elder Wand, the Wicked Witch of the West COVETS Dorothy's Ruby Slippers and Megatron COVETS the All Spark.

33. ANTITHESIS:
Direct opposite; the complete reverse; ANTIPODAL

In the hit movie "Knocked Up," Ben and Allison have ANTITHETICAL lifestyles. Ben is an unemployed slacker who enjoys wasting time with his equally shiftless friends. In contrast, Alison is an ambitious career woman who is highly motivated to work hard and earn a promotion.

In the hit movie "Transformers," Optimus Prime and Megatron represent the ANTIPODES of the cyber world. Optimus Prime is the principled leader of the Autobots. In contrast, Megatron is the utterly ruthless leader of the villainous Decepticons.

34. PROTOTYPE:
An original model

What do the Model T and the Batmobile in "Batman Begins" have in common? Although they are very different vehicles, both were originally designed to be PROTOTYPES. The Model T was invented by Henry

Ford in 1908. It served as the PROTOTYPE for the world's first affordable, mass-produced automobile. The Batmobile was created by Bruce Wayne and Lucius Fox. It served as the PROTOTYPE for a series of armored cars that enabled the Caped Crusader to save Gotham from villainous criminals.

35. ALOOF:
Detached; distant physically or emotionally; reserved; standing near but apart

In *The Great Gatsby*, Fitzgerald initially portrays Jay Gatsby as the ALOOF host of lavish parties given every week at his ornate mansion. Although he is courted by powerful men and beautiful women, Gatsby chooses to remain distant and ALOOF.

In the *Iliad*, Homer states that many accused Zeus of "wanting to give victory to the Trojans." But ZEUS chose to remain ALOOF: "He sat apart in his all-glorious majesty, looking down upon the Trojans, the ships of the Achaeans, the gleam of bronze, and alike upon the slayers and the slain."

36. TRITE, HACKNEYED, BANAL, PLATITUDINOUS:
All mean unoriginal; commonplace; overused; clichéd

Let's pretend that your job is to create a new super-hero for a big-budget, action-adventure movie. What will be your origin story? What powers will your superhero have? There are already so many super-heroes that creating an original character and story will be difficult. It will be all too easy to create

HACKNEYED characters, BANAL plots, and TRITE dialogues. The creators of the movie "Hancock" wanted to avoid all of the usual superhero PLAT-ITUDES. Hancock is the ANTITHESIS (Word 33) of other superheroes. He is an alcoholic, incredibly SARCASTIC (Word 3) and despised by the public. But at least Hancock is not TRITE, HACKNEYED, BANAL or PLATITUDINOUS.

37. ANTECEDENT:
A preceding event; a FORERUNNER

What do the movie "The Omega Man," the Broadway play "Wicked" and ancient Roman flat breads have in common? All there are ANTECEDENTS. The movie "The Omega Man" is the cinematic ANTECEDENT to the hit movie "I Am Legend." The play "Wicked" tells the story that precedes the events in the classic movie "The Wizard of Oz." And ancient Roman flat bread is believed to be the ANTECEDENT or FORERUNNER of modern pizza.

38. PLAUSIBLE:
Believable; credible

IMPLAUSIBLE:
Unbelievable; incredible

Let's play PLAUSIBLE or IMPLAUSIBLE:

In the "Bourne Ultimatum," Jason Bourne successfully breaks into Noah Vosen's heavily guarded top security office and then steals an entire set of classified Blackbriar documents. PLAUSIBLE or IMPLAUSIBLE? PLAUSIBLE because he is Jason Bourne!

In "Live Free or Die Hard," John McClane successfully uses his car as a projectile to shoot down a helicopter. PLAUSIBLE or IMPLAUSIBLE? IMPLAUSIBLE since it is Bruce Willis!

39. PRUDENT:
Careful; cautious; sensible

Would you describe yourself as someone who looks before you leap or as someone who leaps before you look? If you chose the former, you are probably a PRUDENT person who prefers to avoid risks. In the movie, "Along Came Polly," Reuben Feffer was an especially PRUDENT insurance actuary who liked to avoid risks. However, when he caught his bride having an IMPULSIVE (spontaneous) affair with a French scuba instructor, Reuben was forced to reevaluate his overly PRUDENT life.

40. AESTHETIC:
Relating to what is beautiful; an appreciation of what is beautiful or attractive

In "The 40-Year-Old Virgin," Andy's friends tell him his chest hair is not AESTHETICALLY pleasing. In order to rectify the problem, they take him to get his chest waxed. Unfortunately, the result is even uglier, or less AESTHETICALLY pleasing, than before.

41. PARADOX:
A seemingly contradictory statement that nonetheless expresses a truth

In their song "Tearin' Up My Heart," the boys from 'N Sync express a classic PARADOX:

It's tearin' up my heart when I'm with you
But when we are apart, I feel it too
And no matter what I do, I feel the pain
With or without you.

Jennifer Aniston felt the same PARADOX when she summed up how she felt about the breakup of her marriage with Brad Pitt by saying, "When you try to avoid the pain, it creates more pain."

42. ENIGMATIC and INSCRUTABLE:
Mysterious; puzzling; unfathomable; baffling

What do da Vinci's portrait of the Mona Lisa, Fitzgerald's description of Jay Gatsby and J.K. Rowling's portrayal of Snape have in common? All three figures are ENIGMATIC. The Mona Lisa's ENIGMATIC smile has puzzled art lovers for centuries. When *The Great Gatsby* opens, Jay Gatsby is an ENIGMATIC figure whose great wealth and extravagant parties spark endless gossip. And Snape's personality and loyalties remain INSCRUTABLE until the final chapters of *Harry Potter and the Deathly Hallows*.

43. ACQUIESCE:
To comply, agree, give in

In "Pirates of the Caribbean: The Curse of the Black Pearl," Elizabeth Swann and Captain Barbossa conduct negotiations that include "long words." Although he is a "humble pirate," Captain Barbossa does understand the meaning of the word ACQUIESCE:

Elisabeth Swann: Captain Barbossa, I am here to negotiate the cessation of hostilities against Port Royal.

> Captain Barbossa: There be a lot of long words in there, Miss. We're naught but humble pirates. What is it that you want?
>
> Elizabeth Swann: I want you to leave and never come back.
>
> Captain Barbossa: I'm disinclined to ACQUIESCE to your request. Means no!

In short, Captain Barbossa is NOT inclined to ACQUIESCE and comply with Elizabeth's request!

44. NAÏVE:

Unaffected simplicity; lacking worldly expertise; overly CREDULOUS; unsophisticated

What do Sandy ("Grease"), Dorothy ("Wizard of Oz"), Cady ("Mean Girls") and Giselle ("Enchanted") all have in common? They were all NAÏVE characters who were unsophisticated and inclined to be overly CREDULOUS. For example, Cady was originally very NAÏVE when compared with the JADED (spoiled, overindulged) Mean Girls at North Shore High School.

45. AUTONOMOUS:

Independent; not controlled by others

In the movie "Men in Black," Agent Zed explains that MIB is an AUTONOMOUS organization that is "not a part of the system." He goes on to say that MIB is "above the system, over it, beyond it, we are they, we are them, we are the Men in Black."

46. FUTILE:
Completely useless; doomed to failure;
ineffective

In "John Tucker Must Die," Heather, Beth and Carrie repeatedly attempt to humiliate John Tucker. But all of their schemes prove to be FUTILE. Everything they do to embarrass him only seems to increase John Tucker's popularity.

In "The Bourne Ultimatum," Noah Vosen, the Assistant Director of the CIA, repeatedly attempts to kill Jason Bourne. However, Vosen's efforts are FUTILE as Bourne always manages to outwit and outmaneuver the CIA agents sent to assassinate him.

47. INDIGENOUS and ENDEMIC:
Both mean native to an area

Which of the following are Old World plants and animals and which are New World plants and animals: potatoes, tomatoes, maize, sunflowers, cocoa beans, turkeys and buffaloes? Surprisingly, all of these plants and animals are INDIGENOUS or ENDEMIC to the New World!

48. UBIQUITOUS and PREVALENT:
Characterized by being everywhere;
omnipresent; widespread; PERVASIVE

What do cell phones, iPods, Starbucks Coffee Shops and McDonald's fast-food restaurants have in common? They are all UBIQUITOUS - we see them everywhere. Popular fashions are also PERVASIVE. For example, baggy knee-length shorts have completely replaced the once PREVALENT short shorts of the

1970's. From high school b-ballers to WNBA and NBA superstars, long shorts are now UBIQUITOUS.

49. PANDEMIC:
An epidemic that is geographically widespread and affects a large proportion of the population

In the movie "I Am Legend," a man-made virus known as KV triggered a global PANDEMIC that killed almost all of the human population on Earth. While there has never been a real PANDEMIC of this magnitude, virus strains and diseases have caused widespread deaths. In 1347, the Black Plague killed as many as one-third of the people in Europe. In the 16th Century, Spanish conquistadores spread small pox and other diseases that decimated the INDIGENOUS (Word 47) populations in Central America, the Caribbean and Mexico. Our own times have not been immune to epidemics. The 1918 flu PANDEMIC killed 50 to 100 million people or between 2.5 and 5.0 percent of the human population.

50. FORTITUDE:
Strength of mind that allows one to endure pain or adversity with courage

What do Harry Potter, Jason Bourne, and Lt. Colonel Robert Neville have in common? All three demonstrated great FORTITUDE while overcoming formidable obstacles. In "Harry Potter and the Order of the Phoenix," Harry demonstrates great FORTITUDE as he repels two Dementors, resists Dolores Umbridge's tyrannical rule and forms Dumbledore's Army. In

"The Bourne Ultimatum," Jason Bourne displayed great FORTITUDE as he evaded assassins and relentlessly pursued his goal of discovering his true identity. And finally, in the movie "I Am Legend," Lt. Colonel Robert Neville demonstrated great FORTITUDE as he worked tirelessly to find a cure for a deadly virus that almost killed the entire human race.

Testing Your Vocabulary

Each SAT contains 19 sentence completion questions that are primarily a test of your vocabulary. Each sentence completion will always have a key word or phrase that will lead you to the correct answer. Use the vocabulary from Chapter 1 to circle the answer to each of the following 10 sentence completion questions. You'll find answers and explanations on pages 30 to 31.

1. In contrast to the clandestine maneuvers of her associates, Crystal's methods were always open and _____.

    (A) aesthetic
    (B) painstaking
    (C) nostalgic
    (D) aloof
    (E) aboveboard

2. Cell phones seem to be _____, so prevalent are they that they seem to be everywhere.

    (A) anomalies
    (B) anachronistic
    (C) ubiquitous
    (D) autonomous
    (E) obsolete

3. Paradoxically, this successful politician is sometimes very sociable and other times very ___A___.

   (A) aloof
   (B) genial
   (C) trite
   (D) pragmatic
   (E) naïve

4. Uncertainty is an unavoidable part of the stock market; investors should, therefore, learn to accept doubt and tolerate ___d___.

   (A) futility
   (B) pragmatism
   (C) diffidence
   (D) ambiguity
   (E) sarcasm

5. Paleontologists like China's Xu Xing now find themselves in the ___d___ situation of using state-of-the art equipment to analyze prehistoric fossils.

   (A) futile
   (B) nostalgic
   (C) coveted
   (D) paradoxical
   (E) banal

6. Since all the economic indicators were favorable, it seemed like ___*B*___ time to begin the long-awaited project.

    (A) an ambiguous
    (B) an auspicious
    (C) an implausible
    (D) a futile
    (E) a clandestine

7. General MacArthur's bold disregard for popular conventions and time-honored military strategies earned him a reputation for ___*B*___.

    (A) acquiescence
    (B) audacity
    (C) prudence
    (D) indifference
    (E) ambivalence

8. The scientist was both ___*E*___ and _____: she was always careful to test each hypothesis and cautious not to jump to conclusions.

    (A) painstaking .. despondent
    (B) nostalgic .. sentimental
    (C) clandestine .. unconventional
    (D) recalcitrant .. presumptuous
    (E) meticulous .. prudent

9.   Mischa admired his grandparent's ___A___:
     during the Great Depression they lost their jobs
     but they never lost their strength of purpose or
     their dignity.

     (A)   fortitude
     (B)   antecedents
     (C)   anomalies
     (D)   indifference
     (E)   diffidence

10. Parker's _____ nature, evident in his stubborn
     refusal to follow instructions, exasperated and
     ___E___ his teammates and coaches.

     (A)   morose .. mollified
     (B)   obdurate .. charmed
     (C)   sarcastic .. calmed
     (D)   genial .. annoyed
     (E)   recalcitrant .. alienated

Answers and Explanations

1. **E**

   The question asks you to find a word that contrasts with clandestine and is synonymous with open. The correct answer is ABOVEBOARD (Word 17).

2. **C**

   The question asks you to find a word that means prevalent. The correct answer is UBIQUITOUS (Word 48).

3. **A**

   The question asks you to find a word that is the opposite of sociable. The correct answer is ALOOF (Word 35).

4. **D**

   The question asks you to find a word that means uncertain and fits with the phrase "accept doubt." The correct answer is AMBIGUITY (Word 21).

5. **D**

   The question asks you to find a word that satisfies the contradictory but true situation in which Xu Xing uses state-of-the art equipment to analyze prehistoric fossils. The correct answer is PARADOXICAL (Word 41).

6. B

The question asks you to find a word that means "favorable." The correct answer is AUSPICIOUS (Word 26).

7. B

The question asks you to find a word that means a "bold disregard for popular conventions and time-honored military strategies." The correct answer is AUDACITY (Word 9).

8. E

The question asks you to find a first word that means careful and a second word that means cautious. Note that in choice A, painstaking does mean careful, but despondent means very depressed. The correct answers are METICULOUS (Word 8) and PRUDENT (Word 39).

9. A

The question asks you to find a word that means "strength of purpose." The correct answer is FORTITUDE (Word 50).

10. E

The question asks you to find a first word that means "stubborn refusal to follow instructions" and a second word that is synonymous with "exasperate." Note that in choice B, obdurate does mean stubborn but Parker's teammates would not be charmed. The correct answers are RECALCITRANT (Word 15) and ALIENATED.

Chapter 2

CORE VOCABULARY II: 51–100

Chapter 2 continues our goal of helping you learn the 100 Core Vocabulary Words. As in Chapter 1, each of these words was the answer to a Level 3 or Level 4 question. We EXHORT (strongly encourage) you to study hard. As always, our PENCHANT (liking) for vivid pop culture examples will help you learn and remember new words. So don't let the Core Words THWART (frustrate) you. Now is the time to TENACIOUSLY (with great determination) pursue your goal of conquering the SAT. Remember, there is INCONTROVERTIBLE (indisputable) proof that your Critical Reading score will go up as your vocabulary goes up!

51. DIMINUTIVE:
Very small

What do the Munchkins ("Wizard of Oz"), Bilbo and Frodo ("Lord of the Rings"), Mini-Me ("Austin Powers") and the Goblins ("Harry Potter and the Sorcerer's Stone") have in common? They are all DIMINUTIVE.

52. ARCHAIC:
Old-fashioned; out of date; no longer part of contemporary usage

What if someone called you a "sheik" and your girl friend a "sheba?" Would you be flattered or offended? Probably neither since these words are ARCHAIC and thus no longer part of contemporary usage. During the Roaring Twenties, a sheik was a really cool guy and a sheba was a really hot chick. So if you knew what these words meant you would be flattered.

Like words, musicians can also quickly become ARCHAIC. For example, have you ever heard of Grandmaster Flash, Run DMC, and Public Enemy? All three were pioneering rappers whose music and style now seem ARCHAIC. Artists like Lil Wayne and Sean Kingston now have the stage. Of course within a few years the fast-changing music industry will make them seem ARCHAIC.

53. EXHORT:
To encourage; urge; implore; give a pep talk

Are you a member of a team? If so, has your coach ever given your team a pep talk designed to EXHORT you to give it 110 percent and win the game? Taken from the movie "Braveheart," here is William Wallace's famous speech EXHORTING the Scottish troops to stand and fight the English:

> *William Wallace:* What will you do without freedom? Will you fight?
>
> *Soldier:* Against that? No, we will run, and we will live.
>
> *William Wallace:* Aye, fight and you may die. Run, and you'll live. At least for a while. And dying in your beds, many years from now, would you be willing to trade all the days, from this day to that, for one chance, just one chance to come back and tell our enemies that they may take our lives, but they'll never take OUR FREEDOM!

54. ANTIPATHY and ANIMOSITY:
Strong dislike; ill will; the state of DETESTING someone

During the opening scenes of "Remember the Titans," there was a strong ANTIPATHY between Gerry and Julius and between Coach Yoast and Coach Boone. However, this ANTIPATHY turned to friendship as the players and coaches worked together and the team began to win. The players and coaches in "Remember the Titans" successfully overcame their ANIMOSITY. In contrast, Batman and the Joker ("The Dark

Knight") remain mortal enemies who will never overcome their intense ANTIPATHY.

55. GLIB:
Marked by ease and fluency in speaking or writing often to the point of being insincere or deceitful

Lindsay Lohan has more than her share of personal problems. In a recent interview, tycoon Donald Trump GLIBLY advised the actress to "get a new set of parents" as part of her ongoing recovery. Trump's GLIB suggestion infuriated Lindsay's mother, Dina Lohan. She fired back at Trump, reminding him that his own brother died of alcoholism. Dina added, "I am a single mother of four children doing what I can during this difficult time."

Celebrity gossip magazines are not the only place where you can find GLIB remarks. Weather forecasters and used car salesmen are notorious for their GLIB comments. Weather forecasters often make GLIB long-range predictions about storms that never materialize and used car salesmen frequently make GLIB boasts about engine performance.

56. TENACIOUS:
Characterized by holding fast; showing great determination in holding on to something that is valued

What do Jason Bourne ("The Bourne Ultimatum") and Noah Calhoun ("The Notebook") have in common? They both TENACIOUSLY pursued something they desperately wanted. Jason Bourne refused to accept the loss of his identity. He showed great TENACITY in his single-minded attempt to learn who he was. Noah Calhoun loved and lost Allie. He then demonstrated great TENACITY in his attempt to win her back.

57. INDULGENT:

Characterized by excessive generosity; overly tolerant

In the movie, "Mean Girls," Regina George's mother prides herself on being INDULGENT. She proudly tells Regina and Cady, "I just want you to know, if you ever need anything, don't be shy, OK? There are NO rules in the house. I'm not like a 'regular' mom. I'm a 'cool' mom." Mrs. George should have said, "I'm a super INDULGENT mom who lets Regina do anything she wishes."

58. POLARIZE:

To break up into opposing factions or divisive groups

Americans have a long and distinguished record of settling differences by reaching a compromise. However, some issues are so POLARIZING that a compromise is impossible. Before the Civil War, the issue of slavery POLARIZED Americans into two groups: those who defended the South's "peculiar institution" and those who demanded that slavery be abolished. Lincoln eloquently expressed this division when he said, "A house divided against itself cannot stand. I believe this government cannot endure permanently half slave and half free."

59. NEBULOUS:
Vague; cloudy; misty; lacking a fully developed form

Have you read the Epilogue in *Harry Potter and the Deathly Hallows*? If you found it rather vague, then J.K. Rowling achieved her goal. In an interview, Rowling stated that the Epilogue is deliberately "NEBULOUS." She wanted readers to feel as if they were looking at Platform 9 3/4 through the mist, unable to make out exactly who was there and who was not.

60. APROPOS:
Appropriate; fitting; to the point

Some jokes are APROPOS while others are not. It all depends upon the setting and the audience. Here is a joke that was told at an engineering conference. Do you think the joke was APROPOS?

Three engineering students were gathered together discussing possible designers of the human body. One said, "It was a mechanical engineer. Just look at all the joints." Another said, "No, it was an electrical engineer. The nervous system has many thousands of electrical connections." The last one said, "Actually, it must have been a civil engineer. Who else would run a toxic waste pipeline through a recreational area!"

61. FLEETING and EPHEMERAL:
Both mean very brief; lasting for a short time

What do the following groups and their hit songs have in common: "Who Let the Dogs Out?" by Baha Men,

"Stuck In The Middle With You" by Stealers Wheel and "It's Raining Men" by the Weather Girls? All three groups were "one-hit wonders" who had a single hit song and then disappeared. Their popularity was FLEETING. They were EPHEMERAL - here today and gone tomorrow.

62. PENCHANT:
A liking, preference for something, an INCLINATION

Angelina Jolie's well-known PENCHANT for tattoos has had a huge influence on Brad Pitt. Inspired by Angelina, Brad has also developed a PENCHANT for tattoos. Brad's tats include: a Buddhist blessing for son Maddox on his back; Angie's birthday (6 – 4 – 75) on his stomach; and an Ice Age mummy on his arm.

In the movie "Superbad," Seth does not have a PENCHANT for body art. However, when he was a young boy he did have a PENCHANT for drawing pictures of a certain part of the male anatomy!

63. CAPRICIOUS and MERCURIAL:
Very changeable; fickle; characterized by constantly shifting moods

What if you had enough money to buy as many cars as you wished? Would you stick with one model or would you by a variety of cars to reflect your shifting moods? On the MTV show "Cribs," successful rappers, rock stars and professional athletes are often portrayed as CAPRICIOUS individuals who try to match their vehicles with their constantly shifting moods. For example, "The Boss" Rick Ross has a small fleet of cars that include a sophisticated black Mercedes-Benz CL65, a rebellious custom chopper and a decadent Maybach equipped with a lavish entertainment center and costing over $400,000. Ross's collection expresses his MERCURIAL moods and tastes.

64. BOORISH and UNCOUTH:
Vulgar; characterized by crude behavior and deplorable manners

Billy Madison ("Billy Madison"), Ron Burgundy ("Anchorman"), Borat ("Borat") and Ben Stone ("Knocked Up") all demonstrated BOORISH manners and behavior. However, none of these BOORISH characters quite equaled Bluto in "Animal House." In one classic scene, Bluto piled food onto his cafeteria plate while stuffing food in his pockets. He then sat down uninvited at a cafeteria table. Disgusted by Bluto's outrageous appearance and BOORISH manners, Mandy called him a "P-I-G, pig." Undeterred by Mandy's insult, Bluto stuffed mashed potatoes into his mouth and asked Mandy and her incredulous friends "Can you guess what I am?" He then pressed his hands against his cheeks causing the mashed potatoes to spray onto the shocked diners. Pleased with his UNCOUTH antics, Bluto proudly answered his own question by announcing, "I'm a zit, get it!"

65. INDIGNANT:
Characterized by outrage at something that is perceived as unjust

What do Andrew Jackson's supporters in 1824 and Al Gore's supporters in 2000 have in common? Both were INDIGNANT at the outcomes of presidential elections. Following the election of 1824, Andrew Jackson's INDIGNANT supporters accused John Quincy Adams and Henry Clay of stealing the election from Old Hickory. Following the election of 2000, Al Gore's INDIGNANT supporters accused George W. Bush and the U.S. Supreme Court of stealing the election from Gore.

66. INNUENDO:
A veiled reference; an insinuation

Justin Timberlake's song, "Cry Me a River," contains a number of INNUENDOES implying that he broke up with Britney because she cheated on him:

You were my sun,
You were my earth
But you didn't know all the ways I loved you, no
So you took a chance,
And made other plans
But I bet you didn't think they would come crashing down, no
You don't have to say what you did,
I already know, I found out from him
Now there's just no chance, for you and me, there'll never be
And don't it make you sad about it?

67. THWART and STYMIE:
To stop, frustrate, prevent

The Harry Potter saga is filled with dramatic examples illustrating THWART and STYMIE. For example, Lilly Potter's love THWARTED Lord Voldemort's attempt to kill her one-year old son, Harry. In future volumes,

Harry repeatedly THWARTED Lord Voldemort's attempts to kill him.

68. ADROIT and DEFT:
Both mean to have or show great skill

What do James Bond, Indiana Jones and Jack Bauer ("24") have in common? All three are ADROIT at escaping from seemingly impossible situations. Their quick thinking and DEFT use of weapons has enabled all three to THWART (Word 67) the plots of determined villains.

While all three are ADROIT at THWARTING the bad guys, none can compare to the most ADROIT and DEFT crime-fighter of all: Chuck Norris. As everyone knows, Chuck Norris is ADROIT at using a roundhouse kick to escape even the toughest situations. In fact, it is rumored that if someone were DEFT enough to tap the energy from a Chuck Norris roundhouse kick, they could power the entire country of Australia for 44 minutes.

69. ADMONISH:
To earnestly caution; to warn against
(another) to avoid a course of action

First sung in November 1934, "Santa Claus is Coming to Town" celebrates Santa's much anticipated arrival on Christmas eve. However, while Santa may be very MUNIFICENT (Word 222), he is also very VIGILANT (watchful, alert). He keeps a list and he knows "who's naughty or nice." The song earnestly ADMONISHES children to "be good for goodness sake."

70. INCONTROVERTIBLE:
Indisputable; beyond doubt

As the movie "Harry Potter and the Order of the Phoenix" opens, Albus Dumbledore emphatically tells Cornelius Fudge and other Ministry of Magic officials that "the evidence of the Dark Lord's return is IN-CONTROVERTIBLE." Unfortunately Fudge, Dolores Umbridge and other officials are SKEPTICAL (Word 102). Needless to say, as the story unfolds it is clear that Dumbledore is correct and Fudge is ERRONEOUS (wrong).

71. VORACIOUS and RAVENOUS:
A huge appetite that cannot be satisfied; INSATIABLE

What do Homer ("The Simpsons"), Bluto ("Animal House") and Galactus ("Fantastic Four: Rise of the Silver Surfer") have in common? All three have VORACIOUS appetites. Homer has an INSATIABLE appetite for frosted doughnuts. Bluto regularly piles great quantities of food on his plate. And Galactus is a cosmic entity who has a RAVENOUS appetite for planets like Earth that have the potential for supporting life.

72. CALLOUS:
Emotionally hardened; insensitive; unfeeling

In the movie "Mean Girls," the Plastics CALLOUSLY mistreated their classmates. They even kept a "Burn Book" filled with CALLOUS INNUENDOES (Word 66) and sarcastic putdowns.

In Fitzgerald's novel, *The Great Gatsby*, Tom Buchanan CALLOUSLY ruins four lives (Daisy, Gatsby, Myrtle and George) while recklessly pursuing his own selfish pleasures.

73. INTREPID and UNDAUNTED:
Both mean courageous, resolute and fearless

What do Luke Skywalker and Charles Lindbergh have in common? Both were INTREPID pilots who were UNDAUNTED by seemingly impossible odds. In the movie "Star Wars IV," Luke was UNDAUNTED by the Empire's seemingly invincible Death Star. The INTREPID Skywalker destroyed the Death Star with well-aimed proton torpedoes.

The American aviator Charles Lindbergh was also UNDAUNTED by a seemingly impossible task. Despite several attempts, no pilot had successfully flown across the Atlantic. In 1927, the INTREPID Lindbergh electrified the world by flying his single-engine plane, the *Spirit of St. Louis*, from New York to Paris in a grueling 33-hour and 39-minute flight.

74. NONCHALANT:
Having an air of casual indifference; coolly unconcerned

When you are driving, do you slow down for a yellow light and promptly stop for a red light? We hope so. While careful and law-abiding drivers follow these rules of the road, not all drivers do. For example, Italian drivers are famous for their NONCHALANT attitude toward yellow and even red lights. One typical Italian cab driver NONCHALANTLY explained that lights are merely advisory: "Everyone drives through yellow lights and fresh red ones. It is no big deal." Needless to say we hope you will not take such a NONCHALANT attitude.

75. CONVOLUTED:
Winding, twisting, and therefore difficult to understand; intricate

What do the Electoral College and the Bowl Championship Series (BCS) have in common? Both require a CONVOLUTED process to choose a winner. The Electoral College requires a CONVOLUTED process to choose a President and the BCS requires a CONVOLUTED process to choose two football teams to play for the national championship.

76. ITINERANT:
Traveling from place to place; NOT SEDENTARY

During the Great Awakening, George Whitefield and other ITINERANT ministers preached their message of human helplessness and divine OMNIPOTENCE (all powerful) as they toured the colonies. Today, many movie stars also live ITINERANT lives. For example, during the last six years, Angelina Jolie and Brad Pitt have lived in 15 homes all over the world, including Paris, Prague, Los Angeles, New Orleans, Berlin, Namibia, India and New York City. Jolie enjoys her ITINERANT lifestyle and says that it is important to experience a variety of cultures.

77. POIGNANT:
Moving; touching; heartrending

Do you remember the POIGNANT scene in "Remember the Titans" when Julius visited the paralyzed Gerry in the hospital? At first, the nurse refused to allow Julius, who was black, to enter the room saying, "Only kin's allowed in here." But Gerry corrected her saying, "Alice, are you blind? Don't you see the family resemblance? That's my brother." This POIGNANT scene brought tears to the eyes of many viewers.

78. IMPETUS:
A stimulus or encouragement that results in increased activity.

Lord Voldemort's resurrection at the end of *Harry Potter and the Goblet of Fire* provided the IMPETUS for the revival of the Order of the Phoenix and the formation of Dumbledore's Army.

Although it was a failure, Shays' Rebellion alarmed key colonial leaders, thus providing the IMPETUS for calling a convention to revise and strengthen the Articles of Confederation.

79. BUCOLIC and RUSTIC:
Both words refer to charming, unspoiled countryside

Americans have always been proud of our country's great natural beauty. During the early 19th Century, a group of artists known as the Hudson River School specialized in painting the BUCOLIC beauty of

America's unspoiled landscape. Today, many students are attracted to the RUSTIC beauty of campuses located in small towns. For example, one writer described Blacksburg, Virginia, the home of Virginia Tech, as "a quaint, off-the-beaten-track, BUCOLIC college town nestled in the mountains of southwest Virginia."

80. EQUANIMITY:
Calmness; composure; poise

The famous psychologist Sigmund Freud was renowned for his legendary EQUANIMITY. For example, when Freud heard the news that the Nazis were burning his books, he responded with his customary EQUANIMITY. "What progress we are making!" he told his friends. "In the Middle Ages they would have burnt me; nowadays they are content with burning my books."

81. PANACHE and VERVE:
Both mean dash and flamboyance especially in artistic performance or composition; great vigor and energy

During the Middle Ages, proud European military commanders often placed feathers or a plum in their helmet as they rode into battle. Known as a *panache*, the feathers and plumes helped troops identify their commander while also making him an easier target for enemy arrows and bullets. Given the risk, it took real courage for a commander to wear a *panache*.

Today the word PANACHE no longer refers to feathers or a plum. But, PANACHE still retains its sense of VERVE and dash. PANACHE is now most frequently used to refer to entertainers. For example, Andre 3000 of Outkast and Johnny Depp are both renowned for their PANACHE.

82. PROVOCATIVE:
Statements or actions that provoke discussion and stimulate controversy

Prior to World War I, young women aspired to seem modest and maidenly. But that changed during the Roaring Twenties. Once DEMURE (modest) maidens now PROVOCATIVELY proclaimed their new freedom by becoming "flappers." Flappers shocked their elders by dancing the Charleston and wearing one-piece bathing suits. Dismayed by this PROVOCATIVE clothing, officials at some beaches insisted on measuring the length of the bathing suits to make sure that they did not reveal too much of the women's legs. In today's world, this notion of PROVOCATIVE would seem ARCHAIC (Word 52)!

83. PLACID:
Calm or quiet; undisturbed by tumult or disorder; SERENE

What do the Pacific Ocean and the SAT word PLACID have in common? When the legendary explorer Ferdinand Magellan left the Strait of Magellan, he entered an immense and as yet unexplored body of water that he described as a *Mare Pacificum*, or "peaceful sea." The Latin root *plac* means to make calm. Since the SAT word PLACID also contains this root, it too means to be calm or quiet.

84. FORTUITOUS:

An accidental but fortunate occurrence; having unexpected good fortune

In the fall of 1862, the South appeared to be on the verge of victory in the Civil War. Following a brilliant triumph at the Second Battle of Bull Run, General Lee boldly invaded Maryland. In war, however, decisive battles are often determined as much by a FORTUITOUS accident as by a carefully planned strategy. As Lee's army steadily advanced, a Union corporal discovered a bulky envelope lying in the grass near a shade tree. Curious, he picked it up and discovered three cigars wrapped in a piece of paper containing Lee's secret battle plans. This FORTUITOUS discovery played a key role in enabling the Union forces to win a pivotal victory at the Battle of Antietam.

85. DISPEL:

To drive away; scatter; as to DISPEL a misconception

Most football coaches believe that you have to yell and scream at your players in order to win. However, Tony Dungy, the Head Coach of the Indianapolis Colts, disagrees. In his book *Quiet Strength*, Dungy DISPELS this misconception. Dungy does not belittle his players or scream at them. Instead he talks quietly and treats everyone with respect. He guides his players instead of goading them.

86. AMALGAM:
A mixture; blend, combination of different elements

Rap star Ludacris' name is actually an AMALGAM. He combined his birth name Cris and his radio handle Luda to COIN (Word 259) the new name – LUDACRIS!

Similarly, rap star Jay-Z's name is also an AMALGAM. Shawn Carter grew up in Brooklyn near where the J-Z subway line has a stop on Marcy Avenue. Carter's friends nicknamed him "Jazzy." Carter later combined the name of the subway line with his nickname to COIN the new name Jay-Z!

87. VIABLE and FEASIBLE:
Both mean capable of being accomplished; possible

Soaring oil costs and mounting worries about global warming have prompted a search for VIABLE options to gasoline. Many believe that biofuels, such as corn ethanol, are the most FEASIBLE alternative to America's dependence upon imported oil. Indeed, investments in biofuels soared from $5 billion in 1995 to $38 billion in 2005 and are expected to top $110 billion in 2010. But critics argue that corn ethanol is neither VIABLE nor cost effective. By diverting grain from dinner plates to fuel tanks, biofuels are raising world food prices. The grain it takes to fill an SUV tank with ethanol could feed a person for a year.

88. ANGUISH:
Agonizing physical or mental pain; torment

The movie "Batman Begins" opens with a young boy's ANGUISH. Eight-year old Bruce Wayne falls into a cave, where he encounters a swarm of bats. Bruce develops a fear of bats, and later urges his parents to leave an opera featuring bat-like creatures. Outside the theater, Bruce's parents are both killed in a robbery. Filled with ANGUISH, Bruce blames himself for his parents' murder and dedicates himself to seeking revenge by fighting the criminals who control Gotham City. As the Caped Crusader, Batman, Bruce wages a successful fight against crime but must face new and even more ANGUISHING questions: Does his crusade have an end? Can he ever have an ordinary life?

89. INTEMPERATE:
Lacking restraint; excessive

Inimical

TEMPERATE:
Exercising moderation and restraint

INTEMPERATE habits such as smoking, drinking and overeating are INIMICAL (harmful) to good health. In contrast, a TEMPERATE person leads a lifestyle characterized by moderation and self-restraint. Bluto ("Animal House"), Frank "The Tank" ("Old School") and Ben Stone ("Knocked Up") were all fun loving, INTEMPERATE party animals. Compare them with Andy Stitzer's ("The 40-Year-Old Virgin") far more TEMPERATE approach to life.

90. SUPERFICIAL:
Shallow; lacking in depth; concerned with surface appearances

What do Cher ("Clueless") and Daisy Buchanan (*The Great Gatsby*) have in common? Both were SUPERFICIAL. In "Clueless," Josh called Cher "a SUPERFICIAL space cadet" because she lacked direction. Daisy proved to be a SUPERFICIAL person who prized material possessions. For example, she burst into tears when Gatsby showed her his collection of English dress shirts. Gatsby would tragically discover that beneath Daisy's SUPER-FICIAL surface there was only more surface.

91. LAUD, EXTOL, TOUT, ACCLAIM:
All mean to praise; applaud

Have you ever attended a concert in which the announcer introduced a singer or band by asking the audience to "put your hands together for?" Everyone in the audience knows that the word APPLAUD means to praise by expressing approval. But how many in the audience realize that the word appLAUD contains the root word LAUD? Lauds is the morning Church service in which psalms of praise to God are sung. LAUD, EXTOL, TOUT and ACCLAIM all mean to praise.

92. DISMISSIVE:
Showing indifference or disregard; to reject

What do the artist Jackson Pollock, the author J.K. Rowling and the reggae singer and rapper Sean Kingston have in common? All three had to overcome DISMISSIVE critics. Bewildered critics ridiculed

Pollock calling him "Jack the Dripper." INDIFFERENT (Word 10) editors at numerous publishing houses rejected J.K. Rowling's story about a boy wizard named Harry Potter. And Sean Kingston almost quit the music industry after his idols Timbaland and Pharrel dismissed his early recordings.

93. DISPARAGE:

To speak of in a slighting or disrespectful way; belittle

When Donald Trump decided to give disgraced Miss USA, Tara Conner, a second chance after she tearfully asked for forgiveness for excessive partying and drinking, most people praised "The Donald." But talk show host Rosie O'Donnell disagreed. Speaking on the television program "The View," Rosie DISPARAGED Trump calling him a "snake-oil salesman" whose personal affairs made him unfit to be a moral judge. Outraged by Rosie's DISPARAGING remarks, Trump retaliated by calling O'Donnell "an out of control loser." The two continued to trade DISPARAGING insults for several more days.

94. POMPOUS:

Filled with excessive self-importance, pretentious

What do Ms. Darbus ("High School Musical"), Agent Simmons ("Transformers") and Simon Cowell ("American Idol") have in common? All three are POMPOUS. In "High School Musical," drama coach Ms. Darbus POMPOUSLY calls the school stage her "chapel of the arts." In "Transformers," Agent

Simmons POMPOUSLY tells Sam Witwicky, "I ask the questions round here, not you, young man." And in "American Idol," judge Simon Cowell POMPOUSLY describes himself as "indispensable."

95. CRYPTIC:
Having a hidden or AMBIGUOUS (Word 21) meaning; mysterious

As *Harry Potter and the Chamber of Secrets* opens, Dobby delivers this CRYPTIC message to Harry: "Harry Potter must not go back to Hogwarts." But why must Harry stay away from Hogwarts? We don't know, because the message is CRYPTIC. Later in the same book, this CRYPTIC message appears on one of the walls at Hogwarts: "The Chamber of Secrets has been opened. Enemies of the Heir, Beware." Once again, since the message is CRYPTIC we are not sure what it means.

96. SUBTLE:
A gradual change that is difficult to immediately detect

In the movie "Clueless," Josh and Cher initially appear to dislike each other. In fact, Josh calls Cher a "SUPERFICIAL (Word 90) space cadet" and criticizes her for lacking direction. However, as the movie unfolds, there is a SUBTLE change in their relationship as they slowly become closer and closer. A similar SUBTLE change occurs between Veronica Vaughn and Billy Madison. In the beginning, Ms. Vaughn detests Billy for his immature behavior. However, as Billy gradually matures, he begins to win Veronica's respect.

97. DIVISIVE:
Creating disunity and dissension

Although united by a common democratic creed, each generation of Americans has had to confront and then resolve DIVISIVE issues. During the 1960's, the Vietnam War and civil rights were DIVISIVE issues that sparked widespread debate and dissension. The Iraq War and illegal immigration are among the most DIVISIVE issues in America today.

98. CURTAIL:
To cut short or reduce

The rising price of fuel is forcing airlines and average Americans to CURTAIL long-established business and driving practices. In order to offset the soaring price of jet fuel, airlines are CURTAILING service to many cities and many services they used to offer for free, such as checking bags. Meanwhile, American families are trying to save on fuel bills by CURTAILING driving vacations and making less frequent shopping trips. Skyrocketing gas prices are also forcing car-loving American teenagers to CURTAIL the time-honored summer practice of cruising around favorite hangouts. One way to remember CURTAIL is to visualize a tail being cut and thus reduced in size.

99. INNOCUOUS:
Harmless; not likely to give offense or to arouse strong feelings or hostility

Have you ever invited your boyfriend or girlfriend to meet your parents? If so, then you know that there is no such thing as an INNOCUOUS question or answer. For example, in the movie "The Notebook," Allie invites Noah to meet her upper-class parents and some of their wealthy friends. One friend asks Noah what he does for a living. Noah replies that he earns 40 cents an hour working at the local lumberyard. That's not bad for a young man in 1940. But Noah's seemingly INNOCUOUS answer alarms Allie's socially-conscious mother. She concludes that Noah is not good enough for her daughter and that their summer romance must end.

100. DIATRIBE and TIRADE:
A bitter abusive denunciation; a thunderous verbal attack

What do Coach Carter ("Coach Carter"), Coach Gaines ("Friday Night Lights"), and Coach Boone ("Remember the Titans") all have in common? All three coaches were passionate about building character and teamwork. And, if necessary, all three didn't hesitate to deliver a TIRADE when a player failed to follow team rules or perform to the best of his ability. For example, Coach Boone demanded perfection. In one memorable DIATRIBE he insisted, "We will be perfect in every aspect of the game. You drop a pass, you run a mile. You miss a blocking assignment, you run a mile. You fumble the football, and I will break my foot off in your John Brown hind pants and then you will run a mile. Perfection. Let's go to work!"

Testing Your Vocabulary

Each SAT contains 19 sentence completion questions that are primarily a test of your vocabulary. Each sentence completion will always have a key word or phrase that will lead you to the correct answer. Use the vocabulary from Chapters 1 and 2 to circle the answer to each of the following 10 sentence completion questions. You'll find answers and explanations on pages 61 to 62.

1. After his long, exhausting swim, Rajon was _____: he wanted to eat until he could eat no more.

   (A) callous
   (B) pompous
   (C) presumptuous
   (D) voracious
   (E) capricious

2. Serena Williams is often described as having _____ that is apparent in both her dazzling tennis performances and her flamboyant athletic-wear designs.

   (A) an equanimity
   (B) a panache
   (C) a superficiality
   (D) a nonchalance
   (E) a subtlety

3.   Instead of presenting a balanced view of both sides of the issue, the speaker became increasingly _____, insisting that her opponents were both factually inaccurate and morally wrong.

    (A)   enigmatic
    (B)   indignant
    (C)   ravenous
    (D)   placid
    (E)   innocuous

4.   The Post-Modern architectural style is _____: it combines diverse elements including classical columns, Baroque ornamentation and Palladian windows.

    (A)   a diatribe
    (B)   a conjecture
    (C)   an impasse
    (D)   an anachronism
    (E)   an amalgam

5.   The _____ message baffled experts who were unable to decipher its ambiguous meaning.

    (A)   archaic
    (B)   poignant
    (C)   cryptic
    (D)   dismissive
    (E)   fleeting

6.   Boisterous, uncouth and devoid of all manners,
     Artem was widely known for his _____
     behavior.

     (A)   boorish
     (B)   intrepid
     (C)   subtle
     (D)   temperate
     (E)   laudable

7.   The coach's halftime speech to his team was a
     _____, a bitter railing denouncing their inept
     play.

     (A)   diatribe
     (B)   conjecture
     (C)   innuendo
     (D)   evocation
     (E)   antecedent

8.   Hira's supervisor faulted her for turning in a
     _____ proposal that was overly vague and
     lacked a detailed analysis of costs and benefits.

     (A)   morose
     (B)   pompous
     (C)   nebulous
     (D)   viable
     (E)   polarizing

9. The new zoning ordinance provoked such intense debate and caused such partisanship that it was branded the most _____ in the community's long history.

    (A) innocuous
    (B) subtle
    (C) superficial
    (D) archaic
    (E) divisive

10. Emily was renowned for her _____, she remained calm and composed even when confronted with stressful personal problems.

    (A) callousness
    (B) capriciousness
    (C) intemperance
    (D) equanimity
    (E) superficiality

Answers and Explanations

1.   **D**

The question asks you to find a word that is consistent with the phrase "he wanted to eat until he could eat no more." The correct answer is VORACIOUS (Word 71) because a person with a voracious appetite is INSATIABLE.

2.   **B**

The question asks you to find a word that means "dazzling" and "flamboyant." The correct answer is PANACHE (Word 81)

3.   **B**

The question asks you to find a word that is consistent with the phrase "insisting that her opponents were both factually inaccurate and morally wrong." The correct answer is IND-IGNANT (Word 65) because someone who is INDIGNANT is outraged by something that is unjust and morally wrong.

4.   **E**

The question asks you to find a word that means "combines diverse elements." The correct answer is AMALGAM (Word 86).

5.   **C**

The question asks you to find a word that would baffle experts because of its "ambiguous meaning." The correct answer is CRYPTIC (Word 95), because a CRYPTIC message is mysterious and would therefore baffle experts with its ambiguous meaning.

6. A

The question asks you to find a word that means "boisterous, uncouth and devoid of all manners." The correct answer is BOORISH (Word 64).

7. A

The question asks you to find a word that means a bitter denunciation. The correct answer is DIATRIBE (Word 100).

8. C

The question asks you to find a word that means vague and lacking a detailed analysis. The correct answer is NEBULOUS (Word 59).

9. E

The question asks you to find a word that would cause an "intense debate" and spark "partisanship." The correct answer is DIVISIVE (Word 91).

10. D

The question asks you to find a word that means to be calm and composed under stressful conditions. The correct answer is EQUANIMITY (Word 80).

Chapter 3

YOU MEET THE MOST INTERESTING PEOPLE ON THE SAT: 101–130

History is filled with a fascinating array of men and women who have made both enduring contributions and caused great tragedies. This chapter will introduce you to 30 SAT words that describe an astonishing variety of people. For example, you will meet Pharaoh Akhenaton, the ancient world's most famous ICONOCLAST, and Bill Gates, the modern world's most generous PHILANTHROPIST. As you study this chapter you will learn words that will help you describe great orators, notorious traitors, and astute political commentators. That's why we are convinced that you meet the most interesting people on the SAT!

101. CHARLATAN:
A fake; fraud; imposter; cheat

Would you trust the Wizard of Oz, Gilderoy Lockhart (*Harry Potter and the Chamber of Secrets*) or Frank Abagnale Jr. ("Catch Me If You Can")? I hope not. All three of these men were CHARLATANS or imposters who could not be trusted. The Wizard of Oz was a CHARLATAN who tried to trick Dorothy and her friends. Gilderoy Lockhart was a CHARLATAN who interviewed famous wizards and witches and then took credit for their heroic deeds. And Frank Abagnale Jr. was a CHARLATAN who pretended to be an airline pilot and a surgeon.

102. SKEPTIC:
A person who doubts; a skeptic asks questions and lacks faith

In the movie "Men in Black," Edwards was originally a SKEPTIC who did not believe that aliens were actually living in New York City. In "Bruce Almighty," Bruce was originally a SKEPTIC who did not believe that the man he met was really God. And in the movie "Superbad," Seth was originally a SKEPTIC who did not believe Fogell's fake ID, with the name "McLovin" from Hawaii, would work.

103. RHETORICIAN:
An eloquent writer or speaker; a master of rhetoric; the art of speaking and writing

Frederick Douglass, Winston Churchill, Franklin Roosevelt, Martin Luther King Jr., John F. Kennedy and Ronald Reagan were all great RHETORICIANS whose eloquent speeches inspired millions of people. For example, in his inaugural address, President Kennedy challenged Americans by proclaiming, "And so, my fellow Americans: ask not what your country can do for you – ask what you can do for your country."

104. HEDONIST:
A person who believes that pleasure is the chief goal of life

In Ancient Greece, the HEDONISTS urged their followers to "eat, drink, and be merry for tomorrow we die." Although it is a long way from Ancient Greece to the home of rapper Ricky Ross in Miami, the HEDONISTIC principle of pursuing pleasure remains the same. During the tour of his "crib," Ross proudly displayed the interior of his Escalade Maybach, a Cadillac Escalade with the interior of a Maybach. Hooked up with leather seats, plasmas and satellites the interior provides everything a HEDONIST could possibly ask for and more.

105. ASCETIC:
A person who gives up material comforts and leads a life of self-denial, especially as an act of religious devotion

At the age of 29, Prince Siddhartha Gautama left the luxuries of his father's palace and for the next six years adopted an extreme ASCETIC life. For days at a time, he ate only a single grain of rice. His stomach became so empty that, by poking a finger into it, he could touch his backbone. Yet, Gautama gained only pain, not wisdom. He decided to give up extreme ASCETICISM and seek wisdom in other ways. Gautama was successful and soon became known as Buddha, a title meaning "the Enlightened One."

106. RACONTEUR:
A person who excels in telling ANECDOTES

Herodotus was an ancient Greek historian who was a renowned RACONTEUR. Many of the ANECDOTES (Word 203) in the movie "300" are taken from his famous history of the Persian Wars. For example, Herodotus recounts how a Persian officer tried to intimidate the Spartans by declaring that, "A thousand nations of the Persian Empire descend upon you. Our arrows will blot out the sun." UNDAUNTED (Word 73), the Spartan warrior Stelios retorted, "Then we will fight in the shade."

107. ICONOCLAST:
Literally someone who smashes icons. An ICONOCLAST thus attacks and ridicules cherished figures, ideas and institutions

What do the Egyptian pharaoh Akhenaton and the American rapper Lil Wayne have in common? Both are ICONOCLASTS. One of the ancient world's best known ICONOCLASTS, Akhenaton challenged Egypt's longstanding belief in a large number of gods by rejecting polytheism and insisting that Aton was the universal or only god. Now one of hip hops best known ICONOCLASTS, Lil Wayne often ridicules Jay-Z and other rappers, claiming to be the best rapper in the world. As Lil Wayne boasts "I AM HIP HOP!"

108. DILETTANTE:

An amateur or dabbler; a person with a SUPERFICIAL (Word 90) interest in an art or a branch of knowledge

Batman's secret identity is Bruce Wayne, a billionaire businessman who lives in Gotham City. To the world at large, Bruce Wayne is seen as a DILETTANTE who lives off his family's personal fortune and the profits of Wayne Enterprises. Wayne deliberately created the DILETTANTE persona to throw off suspicions of his secret identity. As a DILETTANTE Wayne dabbles in the arts and in various philanthropic causes thus appearing to be both SUPERFICIAL (Word 90) and self-absorbed.

109. PARTISAN:

A person with strong and therefore biased beliefs

Are you pro-life or pro-choice? Do you favor staying the course in Iraq or withdrawing the troops? If you have a strong view or bias on these issues you are a PARTISAN. Remember a PARTISAN speaks up and is NOT INDIFFERENT (Word 10).

Both Michael Moore and Al Gore are PARTISANS. Moore's documentary "Fahrenheit 9/11" is a highly PARTISAN critique of President Bush and the war in Iraq. Gore's documentary "An Inconvenient Truth" is a highly PARTISAN presentation of the causes and consequences of global warming.

110. MENTOR:
An advisor; teacher; guide

What do Aristotle, Obi-Wan Kenobi ("Star Wars"), Regina George ("Mean Girls") and Henri Ducard ("Batman Begins") have in common? All four were MENTORS. Aristotle was a Greek philosopher who served as Alexander the Great's MENTOR. Obi-Wan Kenobi was a Jedi Master who served as Anakin Skywalker's MENTOR. Regina George was a "Mean Girl" who showed Cady how to act like a "Plastic." And Henri Ducard was a leader of the League of Shadows who taught Bruce Wayne martial arts.

111. DEMAGOGUE:
A leader who appeals to the fears, emotions and prejudices of the populace

Adolf Hitler is often cited as the epitome of a DEMA-GOGUE. Hitler rose to power by using impassioned speeches that appealed to the ethnic and nationalistic prejudices of the German people. Hitler exploited, embittered and misled war veterans by blaming their plight on minorities and other convenient scapegoats.

Unfortunately, Americans have not been immune to the impassioned pleas of DEMAGOGUES. During the 1950s, Senator Joseph McCarthy falsely alleged that Communist sympathizers had infiltrated the State Department. As McCarthy's DEMAGOGIC rhetoric grew bolder, he DENOUNCED (Word 176) General George Marshall, former Army Chief of Staff and ex-Secretary of State, as "part of a conspiracy so immense and an infamy so black as to dwarf any previous venture in the history of man."

112. AUTOMATON:

*A self-operating machine; a mindless follower,
a person who acts in a mechanical fashion*

In the Harry Potter series, the Imperius Curse was a spell that causes its victim to fall under the command of the caster. In *Harry Potter and the Deathly Hallows*, the Death Eater Yaxley placed an Imperius Curse on Pius Thickness. When Thickness became Minister of Magic he behaved like an AUTOMATON or mindless follower of Lord Voldemort.

113. RECLUSE:

A person who leads a secluded or solitary life

What do Harper Lee, Sybill Trelawney and Greta Garbo have in common? All four were RECLUSES who wanted to live alone. Although she is the world famous author of *To Kill a Mockingbird,* Harper Lee rarely appears in public. Sybill Trelawney was the Divination professor at Hogwarts who lived alone in the North Tower because she didn't want to "cloud her Inner Eye." And Greta Garbo was a famous actress who summed up what it means to be a RECLUSE when she said: "I want to be alone."

114. BUNGLER: INEPT

*Someone who is clumsy or INEPT; a person
who makes mistakes because of incompetence*

BUNGLERS have been featured in a number of movies and television programs. For example, *The Three Stooges* were a trio of BUNGLERS whose INEPT blunders and madcap antics never failed to leave their fans laughing uproariously. When the movie began, the Mighty Ducks were a group of BUNGLERS who did not know how to play hockey. One of television's most beloved BUNGLERS was Gilligan, the clumsy first mate on "Gilligan's Island."

115. CLAIRVOYANT:
Having the supposed power to see objects and events that cannot be perceived with the five traditional senses; a SEER

Sybill Trelawney was the Divination professor at Hogwarts who claimed to be a CLAIRVOYANT. She used tea leaves and crystal balls to see into the future. Both Harry Potter and Professor Dumbledore were SKEPTICAL (Word 102) about her claim to be a CLAIRVOYANT. In *Harry Potter and the Order of the Phoenix*, Dolores Umbridge fired Sybill for being a CHARLATAN (Word 101). Nonetheless, readers of the Harry Potter series know that Trelawney did make two extremely important and very accurate prophecies.

116. PROGNOSTICATOR:
A person who makes predictions based upon current information and data

Weather forecasters, sports announcers and financial analysts are all PROGNOSTICATORS who use information and data to make predictions and forecasts. It is important to understand the difference between a PROGNOSTICATOR and a CLAIRVOYANT (Word 115). Although both make predictions, a PROGNOSTICATOR uses empirical data that can be collected, seen and studied. In contrast, a CLAIRVOYANT claims to see the future through means other than the five senses.

117. PUNDIT:

An expert commentator; an authority who expresses his or her opinion usually on political issues

On March 18, 2008 Senator Barack Obama gave a much anticipated speech on race in America. As soon as Senator Obama completed his speech, PUNDITS began offering their opinions. Chris Matthews, the host of "Hardball," called it "the best speech ever given on race in this country." Jeff Greenfield, a CBS political PUNDIT, agreed that the "talk about race was exemplary."

PUNDITS, however, are not solely confined to the political arena. For example, Charles Barkley, "Neon" Deon Sanders and Doug Flutie are all former superstars who have now become sports commentators and PUNDITS.

118. ZEALOT:

A very enthusiastic person; a champion; a true believer

William Lloyd Garrison was a ZEALOT who championed the cause of unconditional and immediate abolition. In the first issue of *The Liberator*, Garrison left no doubt as to his intentions when he wrote: "I am in earnest – I will not equivocate – I will not excuse – I will not retreat a single inch – AND I WILL BE HEARD."

119. NEOPHYTE, NOVICE, GREENHORN:
All three are beginners

What do Po ("Kung Fu Panda"), Patch Adams ("Patch Adams"), and Ben Campbell ("21") have in common? All three began their careers as NEOPHYTES. Po was a NEOPHYTE kung fu warrior who ultimately won the respect of Master Shifu and the Furious Five. Patch Adams was a NOVICE intern. And Ben Campbell was a brilliant math student but a GREENHORN blackjack player who had to be trained by Professor Rosa.

120. BENEFACTOR:
A person who makes a gift or bequest; a PATRON

BENEFICIARY:
The recipient of funds, titles, property and other benefits

Nicholas Sparks has achieved international fame by writing romance novels such as *The Notebook* and *A Walk to Remember* that are often set in New Bern, North Carolina. Residents of New Bern also know Sparks as a generous BENEFACTOR and PATRON who has donated nearly $1 million dollars to build a state-of-the-art track and field facility for New Bern High School. As the BENEFICIARIES of this MUNIFICENT (Word 222) gift, the New Bern Bears have become one of North Carolina's top track and field teams. Note that both BENEFACTOR and BENEFICIARY begin with the Latin prefix *bene* which means "good." So a BENEFACTOR, like Nicholas Sparks, gives good gifts and a BENEFICIARY, like New Bern High School, receives good gifts.

121. DISSEMBLER and PREVARICATOR:
Both are liars and deceivers

In "Mean Girls," Regina George was a cunning DIS-SEMBLER who deliberately lied to her friends and to her enemies. In the movie "Pirates of the Caribbean: Curse of the Black Pearl," Captain Barbarossa was a PREVARICATOR who repeatedly lied to Jack Sparrow, Elizabeth Swann and Will Turner.

122. PROPONENT:
One who argues in support of something; an advocate; a champion of a cause

Although America has faced a number of challenging social problems, our nation has always produced leaders who were strong PROPONENTS of reform. For example, during the 19th Century Jane Addams was an outspoken PROPONENT for urban settlement houses. Today, former Vice-President Al Gore is a vigorous PROPONENT of implementing measures that will reduce global warming. One way to remember PROPONENT is to note that the prefix *pro* means to be for something.

123. PRODIGY:
A person with great talent; a young genius

What do Usain Bolt and Michael Phelps have in common? Both are Olympic athletes and both are PRODIGIES. Bolt is a sprinting PRODIGY who earned the title, "The World's Fastest Man," in the 2008 Beijing Olympics. Phelps is a swimming PRODIGY who won an UNPRECEDENTED (Word 249) eight gold medals at the 2008 Beijing Olympics.

Both Bolt and Phelps displayed unusual talent at an early age. For example, Phelps broke his first world record when he was just 15 years old.

124. ORACLE:
A person considered to be a source of wise counsel or prophetic opinions

What do the Pythia and Warren Buffet have in common? Both are ORACLES renowned for their wise counsel and prophetic opinions. The Pythia was the title of the Delphic Oracle, the most important oracle in the classical Greek world. Ancient leaders such as Alexander the Great journeyed to Delphi to listen to the Pythia's prophetic opinions. Known as the "Oracle of Omaha," Warren Buffet is the world's most successful stock market investor. Modern investors often travel to Buffet's home in Omaha, Nebraska to listen to his financial advice and forecasts.

125. MEDIATOR:
A negotiator who attempts to find middle ground

What does the mathematics term MEDIAN have in common with a labor negotiator or MEDIATOR? Both involve finding a middle ground. In math, the MEDIAN is the term in the middle. In a labor negotiation, a MEDIATOR tries to end an IMPASSE (Word 28) between labor and management by finding middle ground that both sides can live with.

MEDIATORS are not limited to labor negotiations. Many high schools have peer MEDIATORS who try to help students resolve their differences. American presidents have sometimes served as MEDIATORS. In 1904, Theodore Roosevelt MEDIATED a peace conference held at Portsmouth, New Hampshire that ended the Russo-Japanese War. Two years later, TR became the first president to receive the Nobel Peace Prize.

126. INSURGENT:

A person who revolts against civil authority or an established government

The United States government used the term INSURGENT as early as 1899 to describe Filipino forces during the Philippine-American War. Today INSURGENT is most widely used to describe terrorists who oppose the American-backed government in Iraq.

127. SYCOPHANT: *Obedient*

A person who seeks favor by flattering people of influence; a TOADY; someone who behaves in an OBSEQUIOUS or servile manner

In the television series "The Simpsons," Waylon Smithers is a fawning SYCOPHANT who behaves in a servile manner toward his boss, Mr. Burns. Here is an example of Smithers behaving like a SYCOPHANT:

Mr. Burns: Smithers, I've been thinking: Is it wrong to cheat to win a million dollar bet?

Smithers: Yes, sir.

Mr. Burns: Let me rephrase that. Is it wrong if I cheat to win a million dollar bet?

Smithers: No, sir. Who would you like killed?

128. STOIC:

A person who is seemingly INDIFFERENT (Word 10) to or unaffected by joy, grief, pleasure, or pain; someone who is impassive and emotionless

What would you do if you scored the winning goal in a championship soccer game? What would you do if your error caused your team to lose a championship baseball game? Most people would be elated to win and dejected to lose. However, a STOIC would remain impassive, showing no emotion in victory or defeat.

Being a STOIC is not easy. It requires great discipline and self-control. For example, tourists to London are familiar with the distinctive bearskin helmets and scarlet uniforms worn by the guards at Buckingham palace. The guards are famous for their ability to STOICALLY endure hot summer weather and hordes of pesky tourists.

129. PHILANTHROPIST:

A person who donates his or her time, money, and reputation to a charitable cause

What do the singer Bono and Microsoft founder Bill Gates have in common? Both are among the world's best-known and foremost PHILANTHROPISTS. As one of the world's leading PHILANTHROPIC performers, Bono has worked tirelessly to raise money for public health programs in Africa. Bill Gates and his wife Melinda are currently the world's most generous PHILANTHROPISTS. Their foundation has given over $30 billion to combat global poverty, find a cure for AIDS, and provide access to information technologies in libraries around the world.

130. RENEGADE:
A disloyal person who betrays his or her cause, religion, or political party

In the movie "Gladiator," Emperor Marcus Aurelius, realizing that he is dying, must choose a successor. Knowing that his son, Commodus, lacks the necessary integrity to lead the Roman Empire, Aurelius chooses General Maximus Decimus Meridius a successful and morally-upstanding military commander. Outraged by his father's decision, Commodus murders his father thus becoming a RENEGADE son. When Commodus asks Maximus for his loyalty, Maximus refuses because he cannot respect the RENEGADE emperor. It is important to note that while the real Commodus was a corrupt emperor, he was not a RENEGADE who killed his father.

Testing Your Vocabulary

Each SAT contains 19 sentence completion questions that are primarily a test of your vocabulary. Each sentence completion will always have a key word or phrase that will lead you to the correct answer. Use the vocabulary from Chapters 1-3 to circle the answer to each of the following 10 sentence completion questions. You'll find answers and explanations on pages 82 to 84.

1. Like a true _____, Drew had a number of constantly shifting interests and hobbies.

    (A) dilettante
    (B) hedonist
    (C) ascetic
    (D) philanthropist
    (E) dissembler

2. Belgian artist James Ensor was often called _____ because he preferred to live and work alone in the attic of his parent's home in Ostend.

    (A) a charlatan
    (B) an automaton
    (C) an iconoclast
    (D) a recluse
    (E) a skeptic

3. Critics accused the used car salesman of being a
    _____ because he tried to dupe customers with
    fraudulent information.

    (A) novice
    (B) charlatan
    (C) prodigy
    (D) sycophant
    (E) clairvoyant

4. Much of Frederick Douglass' prestige and
    influence came from his skill with the spoken
    word; he was a great _____ at a time when
    eloquent oratory was widely _____.

    (A) raconteur .. disparaged
    (B) pundit .. spurned
    (C) rhetorician .. valued
    (D) mediator .. ignored
    (E) prognosticator .. denounced

5. Because Benedict Arnold switched his allegiance
    to the British, patriots branded him a _____,
    and even his new allies justifiably considered
    him an opportunist.

    (A) bungler
    (B) hedonist
    (C) renegade
    (D) demagogue
    (E) oracle

6. As a habitual skeptic, Jordan has always been
    _____ to _____ what others believe to be
    conventional wisdom.

    (A) prone .. misinterpret
    (B) eager .. substantiate
    (C) content .. acknowledge
    (D) reluctant .. doubt
    (E) inclined .. question

7. The _____ prediction was astonishingly
    _____: it offered a bold view of the future that
    no one had foreseen.

    (A) prognosticator's .. unconventional
    (B) partisan's .. obvious
    (C) iconoclast's .. orthodox
    (D) pundit's .. fleeting
    (E) demagogue's prudent

8. The coach was a _____ by nature: she remained
    impassive when her team won and _____ when
    they lost.

    (A) hedonist .. morose
    (B) zealot .. anguished
    (C) stoic .. emotionless
    (D) iconoclast .. genial
    (E) raconteur .. affable

9. As _____, Ashley delighted in disputing
    sacrosanct beliefs, questioning established
    authorities and challenging long-held practices.

    (A) a mediator
    (B) a sycophant
    (C) a mentor
    (D) an iconoclast
    (E) a beneficiary

10. Although Brandon claimed to be neutral, he was clearly a _____ who had strong and biased views on the key issues under consideration.

   (A) partisan
   (B) dilettante
   (C) rhetorician
   (D) skeptic
   (E) bungler

Answers and Explanations

1. **A**

    The question asks you to find a word describing a person who has "constantly shifting interests and hobbies." The correct answer is DILETTANTE (Word 108) because a DILETTANTE is a dabbler who has shifting interests.

2. **D**

    The question asks you to find a word describing a person who "preferred to live and work alone." The correct answer is RECLUSE (Word 113) because a RECLUSE prefers to live a secluded solitary life.

3. **B**

    The question asks you to find a word describing a person who "tried to dupe customers with fraudulent information." The correct answer is CHARLATAN (Word 101) because a CHARLATAN is a fake or fraud who tries to dupe and cheat unsuspecting people.

4. **C**

    The question asks you to find a first word describing Frederick Douglass. You are told that he was an "eloquent" orator who had great "skill with the spoken word." The second work must be positive because Douglass derived great "prestige and influence" from his oratory. The correct answer is RHETORICIAN (Word 103) and VALUED, because a RHETORICIAN is an eloquent speaker and VALUED is a positive second word. Note that answer A is tempting because a RACONTEUR is a great storyteller. However, DISPARAGED (Word 93) is a negative word meaning to belittle or slight.

5. C

The question asks you to find a word describing a person who "switched his allegiance." The correct answer is RENEGADE (Word 130) because a RENEGADE is a traitor or disloyal person.

6. E

The question asks you to find a pair of answers that describe how a "habitual skeptic" would behave. The correct answer is SKEPTIC (Word 102) because a SKEPTIC is a doubter who is inclined to question "conventional beliefs."

7. A

The question asks you to find a first word describing a person who makes predictions and a second word describing those predictions as both "bold" and so farsighted that they had not been "foreseen." The correct answer is PROGNOSTICATOR (Word 116) and UNCONVENTIOANAL (Word 7) because a PROGNOSTICATOR makes predictions and these predictions would be UNCONVENTIONAL because they are both "bold" and unforeseen.

8. C

The question asks you to find a first word describing a coach who is impassive when her team wins and a second word that is consistent with both the first word and impassive. The correct answer is STOIC (Word 128) and EMOTIONLESS because a STOIC is "impassive" and emotionless in both victory and defeat.

9. **D**

The question asks you to find a person who delights in "disputing sacrosanct beliefs, questioning established authorities and challenging long-held practices." The correct answer is ICONOCLAST (Word 107) because an ICONOCLAST attacks cherished ideas and institutions.

10. **A**

The question asks you to find a person who claimed to be neutral but in reality has "strong and biased views." The correct answer is PARTISAN (WORD 109) because a PARTISAN is a person with strongly held and therefore biased views.

Chapter 4

EVERY SAT WORD HAS A HISTORY: 131–155

In 1922 British archaeologist Howard Carter amazed the world by discovering Pharaoh Tutankhamen's tomb. Each of the dazzling artifacts that he unearthed yielded new insights into Egyptian history.

Although we usually don't think of them in this way, words are like historic artifacts. Like the precious jewels Carter found, words also have fascinating histories. ETYMOLOGY is a branch of linguistics that specializes in digging up the origins of words.

Each word in our language has a unique history. The English language contains an especially rich collection of words derived from legends, places, customs and names. These "history-based" words are frequently tested on the SAT.

Our etymological tour will begin in ancient Greece and Rome. We will then explore words from the Middle Ages, European history and literature and American folklore and politics. Our tour will conclude with words from India and the work of Arab astronomers.

A. ANCIENT GREECE

131. DRACONIAN:
Characterized by very strict laws, rules and punishments

Draco was an ancient Athenian ruler who believed that the city-state's haphazard judicial system needed to be reformed. In 621 B.C.E., he issued a comprehensive but very severe new code of laws. Whether trivial or serious, most criminal offenses called for the death penalty. Draco's laws were so severe that they were said to be written not in ink, but in blood.

Today, the word DRACONIAN refers to very strict laws, rules and punishments. For example, the Treaty of Versailles imposed a number of DRACONIAN measures against Germany.

132. LACONIC:
Very brief; concise; SUCCINCT; TERSE

The ancient city-state of Sparta was located in a region of Greece called Laconia. The Spartans were fearless warriors who had little time for long speeches. As a result, they were renowned for being LACONIC or very concise. For example, Philip of Macedon, father of Alexander the Great, sent the Spartans a long list of demands. The LACONIC Spartans sent it back with a one word answer: "No!"

Today, the word LACONIC still means very brief, TERSE. In the movie "The Bourne Ultimatum," for example, Jason Bourne is very SUCCINCT. Here is a TERSE dialogue between Bourne and Marie's brother:

Marie's Brother: Where's my sister?

Jason Bourne: Why don't you sit down?

Marie's Brother: Where is she?

Jason Bourne: She was killed. I'm sorry.

Marie's Brother: How did she die?

Jason Bourne: She was shot. We were together in India. He came for me.

Marie's Brother: Did you kill him?

Jason Bourne: Yes.

133. SPARTAN:
Plain; Simple; AUSTERE

The Spartans were more than just LACONIC. They also prided themselves on being tough warriors who avoided luxuries and led hardy lives. For example, Spartan soldiers lived in army barracks and ate meager servings of a coarse black porridge.

Today, the word SPARTAN still describes a plain life without luxuries. Like the ancient Spartans, American soldiers undergo a rigorous period of training. For example, recruits at the Marine training center at Paris Island must live in SPARTAN barracks and pass a demanding twelve-week training schedule before they can be called United States Marines.

134. HALCYON:
Idyllically calm and peaceful; an untroubled golden time of happiness and tranquility

In Greek mythology, Alcyone was the daughter of Aeolus, god of the winds, and the devoted wife of Ceyx. When Ceyx tragically drowned in a shipwreck, the distraught Alcyone threw herself into the sea. Out of compassion, the gods transformed Alcyone and Ceyx into a pair of kingfishers. The ancient Greeks named this distinctive bird *halkyon* after Alcyone. According to legend, kingfishers built a floating nest on the sea at about the time of the winter solstice in December. To protect their nest, the gods ordered the winds to remain calm for a week before and after the winter solstice. The expression "halcyon days" refers to this period of untroubled peace and tranquility.

Today, HALCYON still refers to a golden time of untroubled happiness and tranquility. In the movie, "The Notebook," Allie and Noah are two carefree teenagers who meet at a local carnival in Seabrook, North Carolina. Although they are from very different backgrounds, the two teenagers are instantly smitten with each other and spend a romantic summer together. These HALCYON days inspired their lifelong love for each other.

135. SOPHISTRY:
A plausible but deliberately misleading or FALLACIOUS argument designed to deceive someone

The Sophists were originally a respected group of ancient Greek philosophers who specialized in teaching rhetoric. However, over time they gained a reputation for their ability to persuade by using clever and often misleading arguments. Today, SOPHISTRY is a negative word that refers to a plausible but deliberately misleading argument.

In the movie, "Animal House," the Deltas are a notorious group of fun-loving misfits who gleefully break campus rules. Outraged by their low grades and wild parties, Dean Wormer holds a hearing to revoke the Delta's charter. UNDAUNTED (Word 73) by Dean Wormer's accusations, Otter resorts to SOPHISTRY in a clever but FUTILE (Word 46) attempt to save the Deltas:

> *"Ladies and gentlemen, I'll be brief. The issue here is not whether we broke a few rules, or took a few liberties with our female party guests – we did. But you can't hold a whole fraternity responsible for the behavior of few sick, twisted individuals. For if you do, then shouldn't we blame the whole fraternity system? And if the whole fraternity system is guilty, then isn't this an indictment of our educational institutions in general? I put it to you – isn't this an indictment of our entire American society? Well, you can do whatever you want to us, but we're not going to sit here and listen to you badmouth the United States of America. Gentlemen!"*

Pleased with his SOPHISTRY, Otter then leads the defiant Deltas out of the chamber as all the fraternity brothers hum the Star-Spangled Banner.

136. CHIMERICAL:
Given to fantastic schemes; existing only as a product of an unchecked imagination

The *Chimera* was one of the most fearsome monsters in Greek mythology. A fire-breathing female, it had the head and body of a lion, a serpent's tail, and a goat's head protruding from its midsection. This frightening combination was unusually fantastic even for the ancient Greeks. The creature's element of unchecked imagination survives in the word CHIMERICAL.

Today, a CHIMERICAL scheme or claim is one that is a product of unrestrained fantasy. For example, according to popular legend, Ponce de Leon discovered Florida while searching for the fabled Fountain of Youth. While the Fountain of Youth proved to be fanciful, we have still have not given up our search for longevity. Fad diets, vitamin supplements and exercise routines all offer claims that have often proved to be CHIMERICAL.

137. OSTRACIZE:
To deliberately exclude from a group

In ancient Athens, an *ostrakon* was a broken fragment or shard from an earthen vessel. The Athenians used these pot shards as ballots in an annual vote to decide who, if anyone, should be banished from their city. Each voter wrote a name on his *ostrakon*. If at least 6,000 votes were cast and, if a majority of them named one man, then that man was banished or OSTRACIZED and had to leave Athens for a year.

Today, the word OSTRACIZE still retains its original meaning of deliberately excluding someone from a group. For example, following World War II, angry French citizens OSTRACIZED people who had collaborated with the Nazis. In Chartres, vigilantes shaved the head of a young woman whose baby was fathered by a German soldier. Crowds of jeering people taunted the OSTRACIZED woman as she walked alone on the city streets.

B.   ANCIENT ROME

138. IMPECUNIOUS:
Poor; penniless; NOT AFFLUENT(Word 221)

When the Romans first settled the lands along the Tiber River, they lacked a metal currency. Nonetheless, Roman farmers did have an ample supply of cattle. As a result, cattle were often used as a measure of wealth. In Latin, *pecus* is the word for cattle. A Roman without a cow or *pecus* was thus IMPECUNIOUS (IM is a prefix meaning NOT) or NOT WEALTHY.

Today, the word IMPECUNIOUS means lacking money and, thus, poor. In the movie "Titanic," Rose fell in love with a handsome but IMPECUNIOUS young artist named Jack Dawson. In the movie "Knocked Up," Ben Stone is an IMPECUNIOUS slacker who has no job and no money. He eats a lot of spaghetti and doesn't own a phone because of "payment complications." Ben has been living for years off a $14,000 settlement check he received after a postal truck ran over his foot. He only has about $900 left.

139. NEFARIOUS:
Extremely wicked; villainous; vile

In ancient Rome, the Latin word *nefarius* referred to a criminal. This unsavory connotation continued over the centuries. Today, the word NEFARIOUS is used to describe someone who is extremely wicked. Darth Vader ("Star Wars"), Lord Voldemort ("Harry Potter") and the Joker ("The Dark Knight") are all NEFARIOUS villains.

140. JOVIAL:
Good-humored; cheerful; JOCULAR

Jupiter was the chief deity of the Roman Empire. The Romans believed that each of their gods possessed particular attributes of character. As the most powerful god, Jupiter was both majestic and authoritative. However, he was also believed to be fun-loving and the source of joy and happiness. Since Jupiter was also known as Jove, the word JOVIAL came to refer to people who have a cheerful, jolly temperament.

Today, JOVIAL still retains its meaning of good-humored, cheerful and JOCULAR. While most people do not associate JOVIAL with Jupiter, they do associate the word with Santa Claus. Often referred to as "JOVIAL old St. Nicholas," Santa Claus is usually presented as a jolly, good-humored man who brings presents to well-behaved children.

C.   MIDDLE AGES

141. DIRGE:
A funeral hymn; a slow mournful musical composition

When medieval Christians gathered to pay their final respects to the deceased, the Church ceremony began with this solemn Latin phrase:

> "Dirige, Domine, Deus meus, in conspectus tuo viam meam."
>
> ("Direct, O Lord my God, my way in thy sight.")

Today, a DIRGE refers to a sad mournful song or hymn of lament. For example, as the Titanic slowly sank its musicians played the DIRGE "Nearer, My God, To Thee" to comfort the desperate souls still on the doomed ship. As POIGNANTLY (Word 77) depicted in the movie, the band played the slow, mournful DIRGE until the very end. They then calmly went down with their ship.

142. MAUDLIN:
Tearful; excessively sentimental

Mary Magdalene played an important and recurring role in the Gospel accounts of Christ's life and death. According to the Gospels, she stood at the foot of the cross, saw Christ laid in the tomb, and was the first recorded witness of the Resurrection. During the 15th Century, artists frequently portrayed Mary Magdalene weeping as Christ was being taken down from the Cross. The word MAUDLIN is an alteration of the name Magdalene. Today MAUDLIN refers to excessively sentimental behavior.

Fans of the Harry Potter novels will recall that Moaning Myrtle lives up to her name by crying incessantly and thus being MAUDLIN. And fans of "The Notebook" will recall that the movie contains many MAUDLIN scenes. For example, did you cry when Noah and Allie died in each other's arms?

D.   EUROPEAN HISTORY AND LITERATURE

143. QUIXOTIC:
Foolishly impractical in the pursuit of ideals; impractical idealism

Miguel de Cervantes' epic novel *Don Quixote* describes the chivalric adventures of the would-be knight Don Quixote. Motivated by chivalric ideals, Don Quixote is determined to undo the wrongs of the world. Blinded by his excited imagination, Don Quixote turns lonely inns into castles and windmills into fearsome giants. After a long series of misadventures, Don Quixote returns home a tired and disillusioned old man. Derived from his name, the modern word QUIXOTIC refers to the foolish and impractical pursuit of noble but unattainable ideals.

In the movie "Little Miss Sunshine," the Hoovers are a dysfunctional family from Albuquerque, New Mexico. Their selfish concerns and petty squabbles are interrupted when seven-year-old Olive learns she has qualified to compete in the "Little Miss Sunshine" beauty pageant in Redondo Beach, California. Despite facing impending bankruptcy, the family departs on a QUIXOTIC journey to reach Redondo Beach and give Olive a chance to make her dream come true.

144. PANDEMONIUM:

A wild uproar; tumult

In Book I of *Paradise Lost*, the fallen Satan commands his heralds to proclaim, "A solemn Councel forthwith to be held/At Pandemonium, the high Capital/Of Satan and his Peers." John Milton COINED (Word 259) this name for the capital of Hell by combining the prefix pan, meaning "all" with the Late Latin word *daemonium*, meaning "evil spirit." As Satan's capital, Pandemonium was a place characterized by noise, confusion and wild uproar.

Today, the word PANDEMONIUM refers to a wild uproar rather than to a specific place. The movie "I Am Legend" vividly portrays the PANDEMONIUM that gripped the residents of New York City as they desperately tried to flee the stricken city. While the PANDEMONIUM portrayed in "I Am Legend" was fictional, residents of New York City living in lower Manhattan experienced an all-too-real PANDEMONIUM as the Trade Towers collapsed on 9/11.

145. MARTINET:

A strict disciplinarian; a person who demands absolute adherence to forms and rules

The French king Louis XIV dreamed of winning glory by expanding France's boundaries to the Rhine River and the Alps. To achieve this goal, Louis and his war minister the Marquis de Louvois created Europe's first professional army. In order to be effective, the new army required strict discipline. Louvois assigned this exacting task to Colonel Jean Martinet. A stern drillmaster, Martinet trained his troops to march in linear formations at exactly 80 paces a minute. The rigid control imposed by Martinet helped transform NOVICE (Word 119) soldiers into highly-disciplined fighting units.

Today, the word MARTINET still refers to a strict disciplinarian. The Marine Drill Sergeants at Paris Island are renowned for being merciless MARTINETS. As readers of Harry Potter are well aware, MARTINETS are not limited to the military. In *Harry Potter and the Order of the Phoenix*, Dolores Umbridge was a MARTINET who tried to impose rigid standards of discipline on the students and faculty at Hogwarts.

146. FIASCO:
A complete failure; a DEBACLE

Venetian glassblowers were renowned for their skill in making intricate glass vases and bowls. Italian etymologists theorize that when a master craftsman discovered a flaw in a piece he was working on, he would turn it into an ordinary bottle to avoid wasting the glass. Since *"far fiasco"* is an Italian phrase meaning "to make a bottle," the bottle would represent a failure and thus a FIASCO.

Today, the word FIASCO still refers to a complete failure of DEBACLE. Most observers believe that the government's initial slow response to Hurricane Katrina transformed a natural disaster into a human-made FIASCO.

147. BOWDLERIZE:

To remove or delete parts of a book, song or other work that are considered offensive

Would you read a story or play containing profanity and sexual references? Probably not. For example, wouldn't you be tempted to substitute "jerk" and "butt" for some less printable words? An English physician, Dr. Thomas Bowdler thought parents should read Shakespeare's plays to their children. Although Shakespeare may be an immortal bard, his plays do contain profanity and suggestive scenes that may not be appropriate for family reading. So in 1818, Bowdler decided to publish a family edition of Shakespeare. In his preface, Bowdler noted that he carefully edited "those words and expressions which cannot, with propriety, be read aloud to a family." Outraged critics attacked Bowdler and COINED (Word 259) the new word BOWDLERIZE to describe the deletion of parts of a book or play that are deemed offensive. It is interesting to note that the BOWDLERIZED edition of Shakespeare proved to be a commercial success, thus vindicating Bowdler's judgment.

The controversy over BOWDLERIZED books did not end with Thomas Bowdler. In her book *The Language Police*, Diane Ravitch argues that American students are compelled to read bland texts that have been BOWDLERIZED by publishers and textbook committees who willingly cut controversial material from their books. For example, an anthology used in Tennessee schools changed "By God!" to "By gum!" and California rejected a reading book because *The Little Engine That Could* was male.

148. GALVANIZE:

To electrify; to stir into action as if with an electric shock

Luigi Galvani (1737–1790) was an Italian professor of physiology whose pioneering work stimulated important research into the nature of electricity. Galvani's name is still associated with electricity.

Today, the word GALVANIZE means to electrify, to stir into action as if with an electric shock. Rosa Park's simple but powerful act of protest GALVANIZED the Montgomery Bus Boycott, thus giving additional IMPETUS (Word 78) to the Civil Rights Movement.

E.   AMERICAN FOLKLORE AND POLITICS

149. PICAYUNE:

Something of small value or importance; petty; trifling

The *New Orleans Times-Picayune* has one of the best known and oddest names of an American newspaper. The word "picayune" originally referred to a small Spanish coin worth about six cents. Back in 1837 the original proprietors of the then *New Orleans Picayune* gave their new paper that name because a copy cost about six cents or one picayune.

Today, the word PICAYUNE refers to something of small value and thus of little importance. New Orleans leaders angrily accused FEMA officials of ignoring urgent problems while they focused on minor details that could best be described as PICAYUNE.

150. GERRYMANDER:
To divide a geographic area into voting districts so as to give unfair advantage to one party in elections

If you think the word GERRYMANDER sounds like the name of a strange political beast, you are right. The name was COINED (Word 259) by combining the word salamander, "a small lizard-like amphibian," with the last name of Elbridge Gerry, a former governor of Massachusetts. Gerry was immortalized in this word because an election district created by members of his party in 1812 looked like a salamander. When the famous artist Gilbert Stuart noticed the oddly-shaped district on a map in a newspaper editor's office, he decorated the outline of the district with a head, wings, and claws and then said to the editor, "That will do for a salamander!" "Gerrymander!" came the reply and a new SAT word was COINED or created.

Today, the word GERRYMANDER still retains its meaning of an oddly-shaped district designed to favor one party. For example, California drew district lines so that two pockets of Republican strength in Los Angeles separated by many miles were connected by a thin strip of coastline. In this way, most Republican voters were assigned to one GERRYMANDERED district.

151. MAVERICK:

An independent individual who does not go along with a group or party, a nonconformist

Samuel A Maverick was one of the early leaders of Texas. He fought for Texas independence, served as mayor of San Antonio and eventually purchased a 385,000 acre ranch. While Maverick's achievements have been forgotten, his name is remembered because of his practice of refusing to brand the cattle on his ranch. These unbranded cattle were soon called *mavericks.*

Today, the meaning of the word MAVERICK has been extended from cattle to people. A MAVERICK is anyone who doesn't follow the common herd. A MAVERICK is thus a nonconformist. For example, in the movie "Top Gun," Lt. Peter Mitchell received the nickname "Mav" because he was a nonconformist who did not always follow the rules.

F. INDIA

152. JUGGERNAUT:

An irresistible force that crushes everything in its path

Jagannath (or "Lord of the World") is an incarnation of the Hindu god Vishnu. In the early 14th century, a Franciscan missionary named Friar Odoric visited India. When he returned to Europe, Odoric published a journal describing how Jagannath's devoted followers placed the god's image on an enormous carriage which they pulled through the streets. According to

Odoric's inaccurate but sensational report, excited worshippers threw themselves under the carriage and were crushed to death. As Odoric's exaggerated story spread across Europe, Jagannath's name was transformed into the new word JUGGERNAUT.

Today, the word JUGGERNAUT refers to an irresistible force that crushes everything in its path. The D-Day assault forces were a JUGGERNAUT that crushed the German defenses.

153. SERENDIPITY:
An accidental but fortunate discovery

Sri Lanka is an island off the southeast coast of India. Known to Arab geographers as Serendip, the exotic island was the setting of a fanciful Persian fairy tale, *The Three Princes of Serendip*. The story and its title inspired the English writer Horace Walpole (1717-1797) to COIN (Word 259) the word *serendipity*. In a letter written in 1754, Walpole explained that *serendipity* refers to the uncanny ability of the three princes to make chance discoveries.

Today, the word SERENDIPITY refers to an accidental but fortunate discovery. When Scottish physician Alexander Fleming went on vacation in 1928, he left a dish smeared with Staphylococcus bacteria on a bench in his laboratory. In his absence, a mold from another lab drifted onto the culture. When Fleming returned, he noticed that the bacteria had not grown where the mold had fallen. Fleming named the active ingredient in the mold penicillin. His SERENDIPITOUS discovery proved to be a WATERSHED

(Word 232) event in modern medicine. Penicillin is still one of the most effective antibiotics used in the world.

G.   ARAB ASTRONOMY

154. ZENITH:
The highest point; the peak; APEX

Arab astronomers called the point of the celestial sphere directly above the observer the *samt*, meaning "way of the head." When Muslims conquered the Iberian Peninsula, many Arabic words entered the Spanish language. Within a short time, the Arabic word *samt* became the Spanish word *zenit*. Over time, *zenit* passed into English and became ZENITH.

Today, the word ZENITH refers to the highest point or peak. On June 12, 1987, President Ronald Reagan spoke for the people of West Berlin and the entire Free World when he called upon Soviet leader Mikhail Gorbachev to "tear down" the Berlin Wall. Reagan's dramatic speech marked the ZENITH of his presidency and the beginning of the end of the Cold War.

155. NADIR:
The lowest point; the bottom

Arab astronomers called the point of the celestial sphere directly under the observer the nazir, or opposite. Thus, the phrase *nazir as-samt* meant "opposite the zenith." With a slight modification, *nazir* entered the English language as NADIR.

Today, the word NADIR is used to describe someone's lowest point. The days following Hurricane Katrina's arrival marked a tragic NADIR for millions of people living in Louisiana, Mississippi, and many Gulf Coast communities.

Testing Your Vocabulary

Each SAT contains 19 sentence completion questions that are primarily a test of your vocabulary. Each sentence completion will always have a key word or phrase that will lead you to the correct answer. Use the vocabulary from Chapters 1-4 to circle the answer to each of the following 10 sentence completion questions. You'll find answers and explanations on pages 107 to 108.

1. The head coach responded to the breach of team rules by instituting unusually strict rules that players felt were too _____.

   (A) cryptic
   (B) diminutive
   (C) draconian
   (D) jocular
   (E) nebulous

2. Outraged editors charged the vice-principal with _____ their work by deleting key parts of a controversial article on teenage drinking.

   (A) coveting
   (B) lauding
   (C) bowdlerizing
   (D) ostracizing
   (E) gerrymandering

3. As a result of the disastrous hurricane, Lindsey was left both _____ and _____: she lost all of her possessions and she faced a seemingly hopeless series of problems.

   (A) affluent .. exuberant
   (B) maudlin .. contemplative
   (C) nostalgic .. laconic
   (D) galvanized .. energized
   (E) impecunious .. desperate

4. Morgan was _____ person, naturally inclined to be tearful and excessively sentimental.

   (A) a quixotic
   (B) a recalcitrant
   (C) an amicable
   (D) a deft
   (E) a maudlin

5. Ryan missed the essay's main theme, focusing instead on trivial details that could only be described as _____.

   (A) picayune
   (B) intemperate
   (C) implausible
   (D) anachronistic
   (E) prodigious

6. Some people alternate between contrasting temperaments; either they are _____ or they are _____.

   (A) nefarious .. wicked
   (B) morose .. despondent
   (C) affable .. genial
   (D) quixotic .. pragmatic
   (E) jovial .. jocular

7. Sydney is best described as a _____: she is an independent person who recognizes that the majority is sometimes wrong.

   (A) martinet
   (B) maverick
   (C) stoic
   (D) charlatan
   (E) ascetic

8. There was _____ when the Jonas Brothers' concert began: fans screamed so loudly that few in the arena could hear the lyrics of their songs.

   (A) serendipity
   (B) sophistry
   (C) pandemonium
   (D) ambivalence
   (E) anguish

9. The new highway proved to be _____: it suffered from expensive cost over-runs and failed to relieve traffic congestion.

   (A) an impasse
   (B) a boon
   (C) a dirge
   (D) a conjecture
   (E) a debacle

10. Charlie looked back on his family's vacation at the lake as _____ time filled with carefree days and untroubled tranquility.

    (A) a halcyon
    (B) an anguished
    (C) a divisive
    (D) an intemperate
    (E) an ambiguous

Answers and Explanations

1. **C**

    The question asks you to find a word that describes the "strict rules" instituted by the head coach. The correct answer is DRACONIAN (Word 131).

2. **C**

    The question asks you to find a word that means "deleting key parts." The correct answer is BOWDLERIZING (Word 147).

3. **E**

    The question asks you to find a first word that describes Lindsey's condition after losing "all of her possessions" and a second word that is consistent with the key word "hopeless." The correct answer is IMPECUNIOUS (Word 138) and DESPERATE.

4. **E**

    The question asks you to find a word that means to be "naturally inclined to be tearful and excessively sentimental." The correct answer is MAUDLIN (Word 142).

5. **A**

    The question asks you to find a word that means "focusing on trivial details." The correct answer is PICAYUNE (Word 149).

6.   D

The question asks you to find a pair of antonyms describing "contrasting temperaments." Choices A, B, C and E are all pairs of synonyms. Only choice D provides a pair of antonyms. The correct answer is therefore QUIXOTIC (WORD 143) and PRAGMATIC (Word 12).

7.   B

The question asks you to find a word describing "an independent person" who doesn't always follow the majority. The correct answer is MAVERICK (Word 151).

8.   C

The question asks you to find a word describing a concert in which fans "screamed so loudly that few could hear the lyrics." The correct answer is PANDEMONIUM (Word 144).

9.   E

The question asks you to find a word describing a highway extension that was expensive, inadequate and noisy. In short, the highway extension was a complete failure. The correct answer is therefore DEBACLE (Word 146).

10.   A

The question asks you to find a word that is consistent with "carefree days and untroubled tranquility." The correct answer is HALCYON (Word 134).

Chapter 5

THE MIGHTY PREFIX WORDS: 156–190

A prefix is a word part placed before a root in order to direct or change the root's meaning. Prefixes are short but mighty. A knowledge of prefixes can help you unlock the meaning of difficult SAT words. Many vocabulary books contain long lists of Latin and Greek prefixes. Many like *anti* (against), *sub* (under), and *multi* (many) are well-known and obvious. Still others like *peri* (around) generate few if any words tested on the SAT. This chapter will focus upon five sets of the most widely-used prefixes on the SAT. Learning them is thus of paramount or vital importance.

A. E AND EX: THE MIGHTY PREFIXES E AND EX TELL YOU THAT THINGS ARE GOING OUT

The prefixes E and EX are UBIQUITOUS (everywhere). You are familiar with them in everyday words such as exit, extinguish, and erase. The prefixes E and EX always mean OUT. Here are seven frequently used SAT words that begin with the prefixes E and EX.

156. EXPUNGE, EXCISE, EXPURGATE:
All three mean to take OUT; delete; remove

In the movie "300," Xerxes threatened to EXPUNGE all memory of Sparta and Leonidas: "Every piece of Greek parchment shall be burned, every Greek historian and every Greek scribe shall have his eyes put out and his thumbs cut off. Ultimately the very name of Sparta or Leonidas will be punishable by death. The world will never know you existed."

Xerxes failed to carry out his threat to EXCISE the names of Sparta and King Leonidas from the historic record. However, a powerful Egyptian Pharaoh, Thutmose III, did succeed in EXPURGATING his mother, Hatshepsut's, name from Egyptian monuments. A female pharaoh, Hatshepsut, reigned for nearly twenty years in the fifteenth century B.C. Possibly motivated by jealousy, Thutmose ruthlessly defaced his mother's monuments and EXPURGATED her name from historic records. All memory of Hatshepsut was lost until nineteenth century Egyptologists rediscovered her monuments and restored her place in history.

157. ECCENTRIC:

Literally OUT of the center; departing from a recognized conventional, or established norm; an odd, UNCONVENTIONAL (Word 7) person

Do you remember Doctor Emmett L. Brown in the "Back to the Future" movies? Doc Brown was the inventor of the DeLorean time machine. Most of the people in Hill Valley regarded him as a strange and ECCENTRIC "mad scientist." Doc Brown did indeed have a number of ECCENTRICITIES. He often enunciated his words with wide-eyed facial expressions and broad gestures. Doc always tried to use a big word rather than a small one. For example, he referred to a dance as a "rhythmic, ceremonial ritual."

158. EXTRICATE:

To get OUT of a difficult situation or entanglement

Have you ever had to EXTRICATE yourself from an embarrassing situation? If so, you are not alone. In the movie "School of Rock," Dewey Finn had to EXTRICATE himself from the embarrassing situation he created by impersonating his friend and claiming to be a certified elementary substitute teacher.

EXTRICATING yourself from a lie is embarrassing. However, being EXTRICATED from an automobile crash can be a matter of life or death. Fortunately, emergency workers have a number of tools specially designed to help EXTRICATE injured people from car wrecks and small spaces. These cutters, spreaders, and rams are collectively called "Jaws of Life."

159. EXEMPLARY:

Standing OUT from the norm; outstanding; worthy of imitation

Have you ever been praised for writing an EXEMP-LARY report, giving an EXEMPLARY answer or designing an EXEMPLARY project? If so, you should be proud of yourself. EXEMPLARY means to be outstanding and thus worthy of imitation. Recording artists and actors are recognized for their EXEMP-LARY performances by receiving a VMA Moonman, a Grammy, or an Oscar. Scientists and writers are honored for their EXEMPLARY work by receiving a Nobel Prize.

160. ENUMERATE:

To count OUT; to list; to tick off the reasons for

What do Thomas Jefferson, the author of the Declaration of Independence, and Kat, the fictional character in "10 Things I Hate About You," have in common? Both felt compelled to ENUMERATE the reasons for an action. In the Declaration of Independence, Jefferson ENUMERATED reasons why the colonies declared their independence from Great Britain. In a poem she read to her literature class, Kat ENUMERATED ten reasons why she claimed to "hate" Patrick.

161. ELUSIVE:

OUT of reach and therefore difficult to catch, define, or describe

According to statistics released by the Center for Disease Control in Atlanta, cancer is second only to heart disease as the leading cause of death among Americans. The disease is responsible for the deaths of about 550,000 Americans each year or approximately 1,500 a day. Despite annual spending of over 5 billion dollars, a cure for cancer still remains ELUSIVE.

162. EXORBITANT:

Literally OUT of orbit and therefore unreasonably expensive

The Lamborghini Murcielago is one of the most EXORBITANT cars in the world. The Murcielago – named, like all Lamborghini's, after a famous bull, can be yours for approximately $313,000. While some may consider this an EXORBITANT price to pay for a car, Los Angeles Lakers superstar Kobe Bryant does not. Kobe gave his wife Vanessa a Murcielago as a gift. However, there was one problem. Vanessa did not know how to drive a manual transmission. No problem! Kobe spent an additional $87,000 having the care converted to an automatic. Kobe could have avoided this EXORBITANT cost by simply teaching Vanessa how to drive a manual transmission!

B.   RE: THE MIGHTY PREFIX RE TELLS YOU THAT THINGS ARE COMING BACK AGAIN AND AGAIN

The prefix RE means BACK or AGAIN. You are familiar with it in everyday words such as REPEAT, REWIND, and REVERSE. Here are ten SAT words that begin with the prefix RE:

163. REPUDIATE, RECANT, RENOUNCE:
All three mean to take BACK; to reject; DISAVOW

"Martin, do you or do you not REPUDIATE these books and the falsehoods they contain?" The place was the Diet of Worms. The time was April 1521. The question posed by the papal legate Johann Eck required an answer. For Martin Luther, the moment of truth had finally arrived. How would Luther respond?

Luther refused to REPUDIATE his words defiantly declaring, "I cannot, I will not RECANT these words. For to do so is to go against conscience. Here I stand!" Luther's courageous refusal to RENOUNCE his beliefs helped spark the Protestant Reformation.

164. REDUNDANCY:
The duplication or repetition of elements to provide a BACKUP in case the primary systems fail

When underwater, scuba divers use a device called a regulator to receive air. Due to the dangers of diving underwater, every system includes a REDUNDANT regulator in case the main one breaks or for another diver to use if they run out of air. This REDUNDANT feature is PRAGMATIC (Word 12) and helps to ensure divers' safety.

165. RELINQUISH:

To give something BACK; to surrender or give BACK a possession, right, or privilege

In the movie, "Enchanted," Queen Narissa's foremost goal is to keep her crown. However, if the marriage between Prince Edward and Giselle takes place, Giselle will become Andalasia's new queen, forcing Narissa to RELINQUISH her crown. The villainous Narissa will do anything to prevent the marriage so that she will not have to RELINQUISH her power.

166. RESILIENT:

To leap BACK; to come BACK from ADVERSITY or misfortune

What do the palm tree, the 2007-2008 New York Giants football team and Bruce Wayne ("Batman Begins") have in common? All three embody RESIL-IENCE in the face of adversity. The palm tree's ability to withstand harsh weather has made it a symbol of RESILIENCE for the Akan peoples of Ghana. The 2007-2008 New York Giants provided an inspiring example of RESILIENCE when they won three straight road playoff games and then came back in the final two minutes of Super Bowl XLII to defeat the previously unbeaten New England Patriots. And in "Batman Begins," Bruce Wayne demonstrates RESIL-IENCE by overcoming the ANGUISHING (Word 88) death of his parents, the DRACONIAN (Word 131) training regime of Henri Ducard and the villainous plots of the League of Shadows.

167. REAFFIRM:

To assert AGAIN; to confirm; state positively

Given at the height of the Cold War, John F. Kennedy's Inaugural Address REAFFIRMED his commitment to freedom when he pledged that America would "pay any price, bear any burden, meet any hardship, support any friend, oppose any foe to assure the survival and success of liberty." Given at the height of the Civil Rights Movement, Dr. King's "I Have A Dream" speech REAFFIRMED his faith in the American dream when he proclaimed, "I have a dream that my four little children will one day live in a nation where they will not be judged by the color of their skin but by the content of their character."

168. RETICENT:

To hold BACK one's thoughts, feelings and personal affairs; restrained or reserved

Have you seen the opening scene in "High School Musical?" While minding their own business at a New Year's Eve party, Troy and Gabriella are randomly chosen to participate in a karaoke contest. Both are RETICENT about participating. But fate has other plans for them. As they soon discover, this is the "start of something new!"

169. REBUFF:

To repel or drive BACK; to bluntly reject

In the movie, "Superman Returns," Lois Lane REBUFFED Superman when she wrote an article entitled, "Why the World Doesn't Need Superman." In the movie "Clueless," Cher claimed that Mr. Hall "brutally REBUFFED" her plea to raise her debate grade. And Amy Winehouse has remained RECALCITRANT (Word 15) as she repeatedly REBUFFS pleas from her family and friends to seek help for her smoking and drug problems.

170. RENOVATE:

To make new AGAIN; restore by repairing and remodeling

Nov is a Latin root meaning "new." RENOVATE thus means to make new again. Hurricane Katrina caused extensive damage in New Orleans and Biloxi, Mississippi. Business and community leaders in both cities have vowed to undertake extensive RENOVAT-ION projects that will restore damaged neighborhoods and revive tourism. For example, in 2007 actor Brad Pitt commissioned 13 architecture firms to submit designs for homes to help RENOVATE New Orleans' IMPOVERISHED (Word 221) Lower Ninth Ward. The project, called *Make It Right*, calls for building 150 affordable, environmentally sound homes by 2010.

171. REJUVENATE:

To make young AGAIN; to restore youthful vigor and appearance

REJUVENATE is an enticing word. Everyone wants to look and feel young. Health spas promise to REJUVENATE exhausted muscles, shampoos prom-ise to REJUVENATE tired hair and herbal medicines promise to REJUVENATE worn-out immune systems. The word REJUVENATE is easy to remember. It is formed by combining the prefix *re* meaning again and the Latin root *juvenis* meaning young. So REJUVENATE literally means to be young again.

172. RESURGENT:
To rise AGAIN; to sweep or surge BACK

Apple Computer was founded by Steve Jobs on April 1, 1976. After great initial success, the company suffered crippling financial losses. As a result, the company's Board of Directors ousted Jobs in 1985. But both Jobs and Apple proved to be RESILIENT (Word 166). Jobs returned to Apple in 1997. Under his leadership, the RESURGENT company introduced a series of revolutionary products that included the iPod and the iPhone. The company's Macintosh computer also experienced a RESURGENCE in popularity when Jobs made the decision to equip it with powerful x86 processors made by Intel.

C. DE: THE MIGHTY PREFIX DE TELLS YOU THAT THINGS ARE HEADED DOWN, DOWN, DOWN

The prefix DE means DOWN. You are familiar with DE in such everyday words as DEMOLISH, DE-CLINE, and DEPRESS. Here are eight SAT words that begin with the prefix DE:

173. DELETERIOUS:
Going DOWN in the sense of having a harmful effect; injurious

What do you think is the fastest growing cause of disease and death in America? The surprising and tragic answer is obesity. As a result of being SEDENT-ARY (lacking physical activity) and practicing unhealthy eating habits, an UNPRECEDENTED (Word 249) number of Americans are carrying excess body weight. This excess weight can have a number of DELETERIOUS effects including increases in heart disease, asthma and diabetes.

174. DECRY:
To put DOWN in the sense of openly condemning; to express strong disapproval

During the 1920's, American novelists such as Sinclair Lewis DECRIED the era's rampant materialism and conformity. Three decades later, Jack Kerouac and other Beat Generation writers also DECRIED sterile middle-class conformity while celebrating spontaneous individualism and creativity.

175. DESPONDENT:
Feeling DOWNCAST; very dejected; FORLORN

What do Danielle ("Ever After") and Giselle ("Enchanted") have in common? Although both Danielle and Giselle ultimately found true love, both also experienced the pain of being DESPONDENT. After being abruptly rejected by Prince Henry, Danielle fled to her home and sat crying on the front step. She was truly DESPONDENT – sad, lonely and deserted by her true love. Giselle also experienced what it is like to be DESPONDENT when a New York City beggar stole her tiara and left her crying alone in the pouring rain.

176. DENOUNCE:
To put DOWN in the sense of a making a formal accusation; to speak against

The pages of history contain a number of inspiring examples of brave individuals who DENOUNCED corruption, tyranny and moral abuses. For example,

Voltaire DENOUNCED the Old Regime, William Lloyd Garrison DENOUNCED slavery, Rachel Carson DENOUNCED the use of chemical pesticides, and Nelson Mandela DENOUNCED apartheid.

177. DEMISE:
To go all the way DOWN in the sense of ending by death; the cessation of existence or activity

What do the dinosaurs and the Whig Party have in common? Both met with a sudden and unexpected DEMISE. Paleontologists now believe that a giant asteroid struck the Earth about 65 million years ago causing the DEMISE of the dinosaurs and many other plants and animals. Historians point out that the Kansas-Nebraska Act of 1854 brought about the final DEMISE of the Whig Party while at the same time sparking the rise of the Republican Party. It is interesting to note that the word DEMISE is formed by combining the prefix *de* meaning down with the Latin root *misi* meaning "to send." So DEMISE literally means "to send down."

178. DEBUNK:
To put DOWN by exposing false and exaggerated claims

Britney Spears' ex-husband, Kevin Federline, aspires to be a successful rapper. Fortunately, Grand Master Larry ("GML"), otherwise known as The Artist Formerly Known As Larry Krieger, totally DEBUNKED K-Fed's hopelessly INEPT (without skill) songs. In his "hit" single, GML rapped:

K-Fed, you COVET wealth and fame
But you got no game

You murder a rhyme
One word at a time
You're easy to DEBUNK
Cause all your rhymes are junk!

179. DERIDE:

To put DOWN with contemptuous jeering; to
ridicule or laugh at

In the movie "Happy Gilmore," Shooter McGavin DE-RIDED Happy as an incompetent NOVICE (Word 119) who did not know how to putt. DERISION is not limited to the movies. New artistic styles have often been DERIDED by both the public and critics. For example, Edouard Manet's painting *Luncheon on the Grass* provoked a storm of scorn and DERISION. Hostile critics DERIDED Manet calling him an "apostle of the ugly and repulsive."

180. DEVOID:

To go DOWN in the sense of being empty;
completely lacking in substance or quality;
BEREFT

What was the worst movie you have ever seen? Why did you select this movie? You probably chose the movie because it was DEVOID of humor, plot and acting. Here is a list of movies that were panned by critics for being DEVOID of all redeeming value: "Battlefield Earth," "Gigli," "Godzilla," "From Justin to Kelly," "Glitter" and "Speed Racer."

D. IM, IN AND IR: THESE MIGHTY LATIN PREFIXES ALL TELL YOU NO OR NOT

The prefixes IM, IN, and IR all mean NO or NOT. You are familiar with these prefixes in everyday words such as IMMATURE, INCOMPETENT and IRREP-LACABLE. Here are six SAT words that begin with the prefixes IM, IN, or IR:

181. IMPECCABLE:
Having NO flaws; perfect

Look closely at the word IMPECCABLE. The prefix IM means no and the Latin verb *peccare* means "to sin." So the word IMPECCABLE literally means to have no sin and thus to be flawless or perfect.

Do you open doors for your girlfriend and say "yes, sir" and "yes, ma-am" when speaking to adults? If so, you are demonstrating IMPECCABLE manners. Do you complete your homework assignments in advance, avoid alcoholic beverages and help your friends by serving as a designated driver? If so, you are dem-onstrating IMPECCABLE judgment. Whether it is manners or judgment, IMPECCABLE always means flawless.

182. IMPLACABLE:
NOT capable of being placated or appeased

In his quest to fight for "truth, justice and the American way," Superman must defeat Lex Luther and other IMPLACABLE foes. Superman is not alone in his struggle against IMPLACABLE villains. Spider-

Man must defeat the Green Goblin, and Batman's most IMPLACABLE enemy is the Joker.

Like superheroes, modern nations can also have IMPLACABLE enemies. For example, the United States and al Qaeda are IMPLACABLE enemies locked in a deadly struggle that cannot be avoided.

183. INEXORABLE:
NOT capable of being stopped; relentless; inevitable

Although it was a luxury liner, the Titanic did not have the advanced warning systems that modern ships have today. The Titanic did have six lookout guards who stood in the crow's nest and kept a vigilant look out for passing icebergs that could endanger the ship. At 11:40 PM, Frederick Fleet suddenly spotted an iceberg directly in the ship's path. Fleet urgently informed the bridge and frantic officers ordered emergency maneuvers. But the ship was traveling too fast. It was on an INEXORABLE course to hit the iceberg. The Titanic sank two hours and forty minutes after Fleet's fateful warning.

184. INCOHERENT:
NOT coherent and therefore lacking organization; lacking logical or meaningful connections

Do you remember Cher's INCOHERENT speech at the beginning of "Clueless?" Here it is in all of its INCOHERENT glory:

> *Mr Hall*: Should all oppressed people be allowed refuge in America? Cher, two minutes.
>
> *Cher*: So okay, like right now for example the Haitians need to come to America. But some people are all what about the strain on our resources. It's like when I had a garden party for my father's birthday, right? I said RSVP because it was a sit-down dinner. But people came that like did not RSVP. So I was like totally upset. I had to dash to the kitchen rearrange the food and squish in some extra place settings. But by the end of the day it was the more the merrier. And so, if the government could just get to the kitchen and re-arrange some things we can certainly party with the Haitians. And in con-clusion may I remind you that it does not say RSVP on the Statue of Liberty.

185. INSURMOUNTABLE:

NOT capable of being surmounted or overcome

Beginning in the 1850's, far-seeing American leaders dreamed of building a transcontinental railroad that would bind the nation together. But SKEPTICS (Word 102) argued that while the railroad was a worthy goal, it would face a series of INSURMOUNTABLE obstacles that included hostile Plains Indians and the towering snow-clogged Sierra Nevada mountains. Crews, which at times included over 15,000 workers, repelled the Indians and blasted tunnels through the mountains. The once INSURMOUNTABLE task was completed when Leland Stanford used a silver sledge-hammer to drive in the golden spike on May 10, 1869.

186. IRREVERENT:

Lacking proper respect or seriousness, disrespectful

The writers of the Simpsons and Comedy Central PUNDIT (Word 117) Stephen Colbert are well-known for their IRREVERENT jokes and witticisms. In the Simpsons movie a message on one of Springfield's church marquees reads, "Thou shalt turn off thy cell phone." In his IRREVERENT book *I am America (And So Can You!)*, Colbert provides a sample of a college essay featuring the overuse of a thesaurus ("the APEX (Word 154), pinnacle, acme, vertex, and ZENITH (Word 154) of my life's experiences") and the false claim that his great-great-uncle's name is on a building at Dartmouth.

E. CIRCU: THIS MIGHTY PREFIX TELLS YOU THAT WHAT GOES AROUND COMES AROUND

The prefix CIRCU means AROUND. You are familiar with it in everyday words such as CIRCUMFERENCE, CIRCUIT, and CIRCULATION. Here are four SAT words that begin with the prefix CIRCU:

187. CIRCUMSPECT:

To look carefully around and therefore to be cautious and careful; PRUDENT

Would you describe yourself as someone who likes to be the first to buy a new electronic device and be the first to wear a new fashion to school? Or do you prefer to take a wait and see approach to new inventions and styles? If you prefer to wait and see, you are being CIRCUMSPECT. A CIRCUMSPECT person prefers to be cautious and look before they leap.

188. CIRCUITOUS:
CIRCULAR and therefore indirect in language, behavior or action

In the movie "National Treasure: Book of Secrets," Benjamin Franklin Gates' great-great grandfather is suddenly implicated as a key conspirator in Abraham Lincoln's death. Determined to prove his ancestor's innocence, Ben follows a chain of clues that takes him on a CIRCUITOUS chase that begins in Paris and then takes him to Buckingham Palace in London, the White House, a secret tunnel under Mount Vernon, the Library of Congress and finally Mount Rushmore. This CIRCUITOUS journey leads Ben and his crew to uncover a number of startling revelations and secrets.

189. CIRCUMVENT:
To circle AROUND and therefore bypass; to avoid by artful maneuvering

During the 1920's, Al Capone and other gangsters built profitable illegal businesses by CIRCUMVENT-ING prohibition laws. Today, illegal businesses continue to CIRCUMVENT our laws. For example, drug lords annually smuggle over 100 tons of cocaine and other illegal drugs into the United States.

It is also possible for a nation to CIRCUMVENT international law. Iran signed the Nuclear Non-

Proliferation Treaty in 1970. Nonetheless, many believe that the Iranian government is now CIRCUM-VENTING its international agreements by secretly developing a program to build nuclear weapons.

190. CIRCUMSCRIBE:

To draw a line AROUND and therefore to narrowly limit or restrict actions

What do Juliet (*Romeo and Juliet*), Janie Crawford (*Their Eyes Were Watching God*) and Viola Hastings ("She's The Man") have in common? Although they lived in very different times and places, all faced restrictions that CIRCUMSCRIBED their freedom. Juliet wanted to live with Romeo but couldn't because her family CIRCUMSCRIBED her freedom by insisting she marry Count Paris. Janie wanted to socialize with a variety of people but couldn't because her husband CIRCUMSCRIBED her freedom by refusing to let her participate in the rich social life that occurred on the front porch of their general store. And Viola wanted to try out for the boys soccer team but couldn't because the coach CIRCUMSCRIBED her freedom by contending that girls aren't good enough to play with boys.

Testing Your Vocabulary

Each SAT contains 19 sentence completion questions that are primarily a test of your vocabulary. Each sentence completion will always have a key word or phrase that will lead you to the correct answer. Use the vocabulary from Chapters 1-5 to circle the answer to each of the following 10 sentence completion questions. You'll find answers and explanations on pages 132 to 134.

1. Unfortunately, the zoo's new pandas were _____: they remained very shy and were reluctant to acknowledge visitors.

    (A) extroverted
    (B) reticent
    (C) incoherent
    (D) irreverent
    (E) itinerant

2. The Mayan's sudden and irrevocable _____ is a long-standing historic _____: over the years, scholars have suggested a number of possible causes including excessive warfare and devastating natural disasters to explain disappearance of Mayan civilization.

    (A) demise .. mystery
    (B) longevity .. enigma
    (C) rebirth .. riddle
    (D) collapse .. myth
    (E) resurgence .. conjecture

3. Scientists warn that the _____ consequences of global warming will not be limited to the deterioration of penguin and polar bear habitats; humans can also expect devastating hurricanes and _____ floods.

    (A) fortuitous .. damaging
    (B) fleeting .. prodigious
    (C) painstaking .. beneficial
    (D) incontrovertible .. innocuous
    (E) deleterious .. destructive

4. Muckrakers like Upton Sinclair and Ida Tarbell _____ the corrupt business practices of early 20th Century robber barons, _____ their unbridled greed and indifferent attitude toward the public good.

    (A) disapproved .. lauding
    (B) extolled .. disparaging
    (C) reaffirmed .. deriding
    (D) celebrated .. censuring
    (E) decried .. denouncing

5. Cautious, conventional, and always careful to follow procedures, Matthew is the very model of a _____ government bureaucrat.

    (A) audacious
    (B) resilient
    (C) circumspect
    (D) sardonic
    (E) maudlin

6. Claire was both envied and renowned for her faultless manners, refined taste and _____ sense of decorum.

(A) vulgar
(B) incoherent
(C) impeccable
(D) obsolete
(E) irreverent

7. Far from draining their energy, the challenge posed by the Tournament of Champions seems to have _____ the coach and his previously indifferent team.

(A) rejuvenated
(B) polarized
(C) circumscribed
(D) depleted
(E) bored

8. What is the most inspiring about Professor DeMarco's portrayal of Venetian life is the _____ of the human spirit, the force that has sustained   the island-city through adversity and always remains undaunted.

(A) divisiveness
(B) resilience
(C) superficiality
(D) reticence
(E) callousness

9. The debate between the candidates was animated but _____, since the speakers needlessly repeated campaign slogans and innocuous promises.

    (A) eccentric
    (B) sarcastic
    (C) unconventional
    (D) serene
    (E) redundant

10. Jessica's report was criticized for being both _____ and _____: it was poorly organized and overly vague.

    (A) meticulous .. ambiguous
    (B) circuitous .. adroit
    (C) incoherent .. nebulous
    (D) glib .. poignant
    (E) inexorable .. dismissive

Answers and Explanations

1. **B**

    The question asks you to find a word that best describes "shy" pandas that are "reluctant to acknowledge visitors." The correct answer is RETICENT (Word 168).

2. **A**

    The question asks you to find a pair of words that are consistent with the Mayan's "disappearance" and the fact that scholars still cannot explain why they vanished. The correct answer is DEMISE (Word 177) and MYSTERY.

3. **E**

    The question asks you to find a pair of negative words that are consistent with the key words "deterioration" and "devastating." The correct answer is DELETERIOUS (Word 173) and DESTRUCTIVE. Note that DESTRUCTIVE is consistent with "devastating" and that the consequences of global warming are DELETERIOUS for both animals and humans.

4. **E**

    The question asks you to find a pair of words describing how muckrakers would respond to robber barons who are described as "corrupt," greedy and "indifferent to the public good." Choices A, B, C, and D all include both positive and negative words. Since the sentence calls for a logically consistent pair of negative words, the correct answer is DECRIED (WORD 174) and DENOUNCING (Word 176).

5.   C

The question asks you to find a word that describes a bureaucrat who is "cautious, conventional, and always careful to follow procedures." The correct answer is CIRCUMSPECT (Word 187).

6.   C

The question asks you to find a word that is consistent with having "faultless manner" and "refined taste." The correct answer is IMPECCABLE (Word 181).

7.   A

The question asks you to find a word that describes the impact the Tournament of Champions had upon a "coach and his previously indifferent team." It is important to note that the competition did not "drain their energy." The correct answer is REJUVENATE (Word 171) since it contrasts with both the phrases "draining their energy" and "previously indifferent."

8.   B

The question asks you to find a word that best describes the spirit of the Venetians. You are told that this spirit or force sustained the Venetians through "adversity and always remains un-daunted." The correct answer is RESILIENCE (Word 166).

9.   E

The question asks you to find a word that means "needlessly repeated." The correct answer is REDUNDANT (Word 164).

10. C

The question asks you to find a first word that means "poorly organized" and a second word that means "overly vague." The correct answer is INCOHERENT (Word 184) and NEBULOUS (Word 59).

Fast Review

Quick Definitions

Volume 1 contains 190 words each of which is illustrated with vivid pop culture and historic examples. The Fast Review is designed to provide you with an easy and efficient way to review each of these words. I recommend that you put a check beside each word that you know. That way you can quickly identify the words you are having trouble remembering. Focus on each hard to remember word by going over its definition, reviewing its examples and by trying to come up with your own memory tip. For example, Word 50, FORTITUDE begins with the word FORT. Now visualize a military fort. Is your fort manned by troops and protected by cannons? Good! Since FORT means strong, FORTITUDE also includes the idea of strength. FORTITUDE refers to the strength of mind that enables a person to encounter danger or adversity with courage.

Good luck with your review. Remember, don't expect to learn all of these words at once. Frequent repetition is the best way to learn and remember new words.

● = Not in '10

CHAPTER 1: CORE VOCABULARY – PART I

1. AMBIVALENT – mixed feelings
2. ANOMALY and ATYPICAL – a deviation from the norm
3. SARCASTIC and SARDONIC – derisive mocking comments
4. DEARTH and PAUCITY – a scarcity or shortage
5. PRATTLE – to babble incessantly
6. WRY – dry humor
7. UNCONVENTIONAL and UNORTHODOX – not ordinary or typical
8. PAINSTAKING and METICULOUS – very exacting, highly detailed
9. AUDACIOUS – very bold; daring
10. INDIFFERENT and APATHETIC – lack of interest or concern
11. DIFFIDENT – lacking self-confidence
12. PRAGMATIC – practical, sensible
13. EVOCATION – an imaginative re-creation
14. PRESUMPTUOUS – overbearing; impertinently bold
15. RECALCITRANT and OBDURATE – very stubborn, defiant
16. BOON – a timely benefit
    BANE – a source of harm
17. CLANDESTINE and SURREPTITIOUS – secretive; not aboveboard; covert
18. AFFABLE, AMIABLE, GENIAL, GREGARIOUS – agreeable; friendly

19. CONFOUNDED and PERPLEXED – puzzled; confused

20. PRODIGIOUS – enormous; massive

21. AMBIGUOUS – unclear; not definitive

22. REPROACH and CENSURE – to scold; rebuke

23. NOSTALGIA – a sentimental longing for the past

24. CONJECTURE and SUPPOSITION – an inference

25. OBSOLETE – no longer in use

26. AUSPICIOUS – very favorable

27. MOROSE and DESPONDENT – very depressed

28. IMPASSE – failure to reach an agreement

29. ANACHRONISM – not in the proper time period

30. BELIE – to give a false impression

31. MITIGATE, MOLLIFY, ASSUAGE, ALLEVIATE – to ease; relieve; lessen

32. COVET – to strongly desire; to crave

33. ANTITHESIS and ANTIPODAL – direct opposite

34. PROTOTYPE – an original model

35. ALOOF – detached; reserved

36. TRITE, HACKNEYED, BANAL, PLATITUDINOUS - commonplace

37. ANTECEDENT and FORERUNNER – a preceding event

38. PLAUSIBLE - believable
    IMPLAUSIBLE – not believable

39. PRUDENT – careful; cautious

40. AESTHETIC – an appreciation of what is beautiful or attractive

41. PARADOX – a seeming contradiction that expresses a truth

42. ENIGMATIC and INSCRUTABLE – mysterious; baffling

43. ACQUIESCE – to comply

44. NAÏVE and CREDULOUS – unsophisticated

45. AUTONOMOUS - independent

46. FUTILE – doomed to failure

47. INDIGENOUS and ENDEMIC – native to an area

48. UBIQUITOUS and PREVALENT – everywhere; widespread; prevalent

49. PANDEMIC – widespread epidemic

50. FORTITUDE – strength of mind

CHAPTER 2: CORE VOCABULARY – PART II

51. DIMINUTIVE – very small
52. ARCHAIC – out of date; old-fashioned
53. EXHORT – to strongly encourage
54. ANTIPATHY and ANIMOSITY – strong dislike
55. GLIB – fluent but insincere
56. TENACIOUS – showing great determination
57. INDULGENT – overly tolerant
58. POLARIZE – to break into opposing factions
59. NEBULOUS – vague; lacking a fully developed form
60. APROPOS - appropriate
61. FLEETING and EPHEMERAL – very brief; short lived
62. PENCHANT – a preference for something; an inclination
63. CAPRICIOUS and MERCURIAL – fickle; constantly shifting moods
64. BOORISH and UNCOUTH – vulgar; crude
65. INDIGNANT – outrage at something that is unjust
66. INNUENDO – a veiled reference
67. THWART and STYMIE – to stop; frustrate
68. ADROIT and DEFT - skillful
69. ADMONISH – to earnestly caution
70. INCONTROVERTIBLE – indisputable; beyond doubt
71. VORACIOUS and RAVENOUS – a huge appetite; cannot be satisfied; insatiable

72. CALLOUS - insensitive
73. INTREPID and UNDAUNTED – fearless; courageous
74. NONCHALANT – casual indifference
75. CONVOLUTED – twisted; intricate
76. ITINERANT – mobile; not sedentary
77. POIGNANT – touching; heartrending
78. IMPETUS – a stimulus or encouragement
79. BUCOLIC and RUSTIC – pastoral; charmingly rural
80. EQUANIMITY – calmness; composure
81. PANACHE and VERVE – dash and flamboyant
82. PROVOCATIVE – provokes controversy
83. PLACID and SERENE – very calm; quiet
84. FORTUITOUS – an accidental but fortunate occurrence
85. DISPEL – to drive away; scatter
86. AMALGAM – a mixture; combination of different elements
87. VIABLE and FEASIBLE - possible
88. ANGUISH – agonizing physical or mental pain
89. INTEMPERATE – lacking restraint; excessive
    TEMPERATE – exercising moderation
90. SUPERFICIAL – shallow; lacking depth
91. LAUD, EXTOL, TOUT, ACCLAIM – praise; applaud
92. DISMISSIVE – to reject; disregard
93. DISPARAGE – belittle; slight
94. POMPOUS – pretentious; filled with excessive self-importance

95. CRYPTIC – mysterious; having a hidden meaning

96. SUBTLE – a gradual almost imperceptible change

97. DIVISIVE – creating disunity and dissension

98. CURTAIL – to cut short or reduce

99. INNOCUOUS - harmless

100. DIATRIBE and TIRADE – a bitter denunciation

CHAPTER 3: YOU MEET THE MOST INTERESTING PEOPLE ON THE SAT

101. CHARLATAN – a fake; a fraud; a cheat

102. SKEPTIC – a doubter

103. RHETORICIAN – an eloquent writer or speaker

104. HEDONIST – seeker of pleasure

105. ASCETIC – a person who leads a life of self-denial

106. RACONTEUR – a person who excels in telling anecdotes

107. ICONOCLAST – someone who attacks cherished ideas and institutions

108. DILETTANTE – an amateur or dabbler

109. PARTISAN – a person with biased beliefs

110. MENTOR – a teacher; a guide; an advisor

111. DEMAGOGUE – a speaker who appeals to emotions, fears or prejudices

112. AUTOMATON – a person who acts in a mechanical fashion; a mindless follower

113. RECLUSE – a person who leads a secluded, solitary life

114. BUNGLER – a clumsy or inept person

115. CLAIRVOYANT – a person who uses intuition to see into the future; a seer

116. PROGNOSTICATOR – a person who makes predictions based upon data

117. PUNDIT – a professional commentator

118. ZEALOT – a very enthusiastic person

119. NEOPHYTE, NOVICE and GREENHORN – a beginner

120. BENEFACTOR – a person who gives gifts
     BENEFICIARY – a person who receives benefits
121. DISSEMBLER and PREVARICATOR – a liar; deceiver
122. PROPONENT – a champion of a cause
123. PRODIGY – a young genius
124. ORACLE – a person who is a source of wise counsel and prophetic advice
125. MEDIATOR – a negotiator who attempts to find middle ground
126. INSURGENT – a person who revolts against established authorities
127. SYCOPHANT and OBSEQUIOUS – a person who behaves in a servile manner; a toady
128. STOIC – a person who is impassive and emotionless
129. PHILANTHROPIST – a person who donates to a charitable cause
130. RENEGADE – a disloyal person

CHAPTER 4: EVERY SAT WORD HAS A HISTORY

131. DRACONIAN – very strict laws and rules
132. LACONIC, SUCCINCT, TERSE – very concise; brief
133. SPARTAN and AUSTERE – plain; simple
134. HALCYON – idyllically calm and tranquil
135. SOPHISTRY – a deliberately misleading argument
136. CHIMERICAL – a fantastic scheme; unchecked imagination
137. OSTRACIZE – to deliberately exclude from a group
138. IMPECUNIOUS – poor; penniless; not affluent
139. NEFARIOUS – extremely wicked; vile
140. JOVIAL and JOCULAR – good-humored; cheerful
141. DIRGE – a funeral hymn; mournful music
142. MAUDLIN – excessively sentimental
143. QUIXOTIC – foolishly impractical
144. PANDEMONIUM – a wild uproar; tumult
145. MARTINET – a strict disciplinarian
146. FIASCO and DEBACLE – a complete failure
147. BOWDLERIZE – to remove or delete objectionable parts of a book
148. GALVANIZE – to electrify; stir into action
149. PICAYUNE – something of small value; petty; trifling
150. GERRYMANDER – to divide a district so as to give one side an advantage

151. MAVERICK – an independent person
152. JUGGERNAUT – an irresistible force
153. SERENDIPITY – an accidental but fortunate discovery
154. ZENITH and APEX – the highest point
155. NADIR – the lowest point

CHAPTER 5: THE MIGHTY PREFIXES

156. EXPUNGE, EXCISE, EXPURGATE – delete; remove

157. ECCENTRIC – an odd, unconventional person

158. EXTRICATE – to get out of a difficult situation

159. EXEMPLARY - outstanding

160. ENUMERATE – to list; to tick off

161. ELUSIVE – out of reach; difficult to catch

162. EXORBITANT – unreasonably expensive

163. REPUDIATE, RECANT, RENOUNCE – to take back; disavow

164. REDUNDANCY – duplication or repetition

165. RELINQUISH – to give something back

166. RESILIENT – to bounce back

167. REAFFIRM – to assert again

168. RETICENT – to hold back one's thoughts and feelings

169. REBUFF – to repel or drive back; to bluntly reject

170. RENOVATE – to make new again

171. REJUVENATE – to make young again

172. RESURGENT – to rise again; surge back

173. DELETERIOUS – harmful; injurious

174. DECRY – to express strong disapproval

175. DESPONDENT and FORLORN – feeling downcast; dejected

176. DENOUNCE – to speak against

177. DEMISE – the final ending of something; the downfall

178. DEBUNK – to put down by exposing false claims
179. DERIDE – to put down with contemptuous jeering
180. DEVOID – completely lacking in something
181. IMPECCABLE – faultless; perfect
182. IMPLACABLE – not capable of being appeased
183. INEXORABLE – relentless, unstoppable
184. INCOHERENT – lacking organization or logic
185. INSURMOUNTABLE – not capable of being overcome
186. IRREVERENT – lacking proper respect; disrespectful
187. CIRCUMSPECT and PRUDENT – cautious; careful
188. CIRCUITOUS – circular and therefore indirect
189. CIRCUMVENT – to avoid by artful maneuvering
190. CIRCUMSCRIBE – to narrowly restrict; to limit action; to draw a line around

Index

Word	Page

INDEX

Word	Page

Word	*Page*

INDEX

Word	Page

INDEX

Word	*Page*

Word	Page

Printed in the United States
221403BV00001B/89/P